Even the Brave Falter

Even the Brave Falter

E. D. SMITH

ROBERT HALE LIMITED
LONDON

ISBN 0 7091 6819 5

Robert Hale Limited
Clerkenwell House
Clerkenwell Green
London, EC1R 0HT

Printed in Great Britain by
Lowe & Brydone Printers Limited, Thetford, Norfolk.
Bound by Weatherby Woolnough Limited, Northants.

CONTENTS

PREFACE

This story is a true one based on a diary, the letters sent to my parents and the accounts I wrote after the Second World War was over. Nevertheless, I cannot deny that there have been gaps in the documents and, as a consequence, I have had to rely on a middle-aged memory. Recollections of many incidents have been diminished by the passing years : at times it has been difficult to separate fact from fiction.

My account is not an unofficial history of a Gurkha battalion and its members. Far from it : it contains thoughts, impressions, and memories of a young subaltern as he learnt how to lead Gurkha soldiers in times of stress and peril. The characters in the book all lived in 1944, albeit under other names, and fought in Italy—some were to die before the end of that year.

The heroism of the cheerful and gallant Gurkhas of Nepal has attracted countless admirers and several books have paid testimony to their bravery in action while serving the British Crown for over one hundred and fifty years.

Nevertheless, the picture presented to the world has been a trifle unbalanced, as if all the tough soldiers from Nepal were supermen. While it is true that a gallant few have won the Victoria Cross, so, too, have Australians, New Zealanders, Canadians, Indians as well as citizens from our own country. The VCs, and countless others, found the strength to live up to the motto, an ideal that has been passed from father to son in the mountain villages of Nepal. But many others have faltered when faced with death in battle.

My story demonstrates that courage is unpredictable. The riflemen who turned and ran on Monte Grillo, next day held fast and fought like lions : the same company of soldiers temporarily lost all fighting spirit below Tavoleto, only to be transformed into the band of fanatical furies who stormed and captured the village against all odds. Death claimed many of them that night ; those that died had obeyed the motto, " Kaphar hunne bhanda marnu ramro ".

I am proud to have shared so many experiences in 1944 with the Gurkha soldiers of my Regiment. The cheerfulness and loyalty shown in battle, even when many of them were afraid, is something that I can never forget.

" Never had a country more faithful friends than you ".

Sidmouth/London

July 1975 to March 1976.

Chapter 1

"IN AT THE DEEP END"

THE night before we landed at Taranto, in South Italy, there was a boisterous rowdy sing song in the first class lounge on the 'Empire Pride'. One of the most popular ditties was :

'I don't want to join the Army,
I don't want to go to war.
I'd rather hang around,
Piccadilly Underground,
living on the earnings of a high-born lady.
I don't want a bullet up my ....'

The various parts of the body that could have been shot away made no difference to the hearty rendering of that old song. There were no women on the troop-ship but there was wine and plenty of song.

But irrespective of how much alcohol we had consumed the truth of the matter was that we did want to go to war. Not to be heroes, nor to kill our fellow men, nor to risk, as the song put it, having our bollocks shot away, but, as officers of the 7th Gurkha Rifles, to accompany our Battalion where ever it went. And the Battalion was part of 4th Indian Division, due to join the American Fifth Army shortly.

Next day, after we landed, six of us were brought down to earth with a bump. The number of British officers with each battalion had been reduced so that those surplus to establishment were to stay behind in the reinforcement camp. Deeply disappointed, we stood in front of old man B, our Colonel. In his fussy, hesitant way he explained why we were being left 'out of battle'. Inevitably, in each of our minds was the thought : Yes, but why me ? He ended by saying : "I realise that you are disappointed. If I was in your shoes I would be, too, but let me reassure you that within weeks, possibly even days, you will all be joining us. I am not saying this to cheer you up : the news from Cassino is gloomy and casualties will be heavy—unfortunately".

I had never heard of Cassino before. Nevertheless after the Battalion had moved off, it became apparent from official communiques and gossip in the officers' mess that a bloody struggle for possession of the Monastery on Monte Cassino, above the town, had developed into a slogging match—a deadlock had resulted.

I wrote to my mother on 3 January and tried to let her know a little about what was happening without incurring the displeasure of the censor. All letters were liable to be opened. In time we accepted censorship although the more ardent writers, who were keeping the flames of love alive by mail, had to refashion erotic thoughts into words which they knew would be read not only by their beloved but by the platoon or company officer, the unit censor. I had no problem, of course, writing to my mother. 'As you can see I have eventually ended up in Italy—" land of sunshine and romance''. Actually the country around here is very pleasant, not unlike England in character or climate. The people are just as I pictured they would be—excitable, very happy or quite the opposite, very theatrical. I went for a walk this morning across the country and sat down on a mound. The war seemed of the past with the blue sky and sea, the green country dotted with white houses and in the foreground, a lad with his flock of sheep. After a few minutes he was merrily playing a mouthorgan, only stopping to sing a few choice pieces of opera. Even the sheep seemed to be more musical than our solid English variety. It was the first real peace that I have had for a month or two. The army seemed far behind with its inevitable worries, parades or regulations. Dozens of aeroplanes brought the dreaming me back to reality and peace was ended !'.

Two weeks later another of my letters was to bemoan that, ' Life in this camp is not what may be termed as over exciting—training never is, however. The food and comfort generally of the Mess has been improving, a fact which makes life more pleasant. We are in tents which have had a busy time resisting the strong cold winds that have been sweeping across the country. I shall be glad when the glorious Italian sunshine arrives—I can't imagine why people come to Italy in peace time to escape the rigours of our English climate !'

Unbeknown to me the future was beckoning. My mother was to read a few days later : ' I am writing this a lttle earlier than I might have done normally, the chief reason being that I am moving today or tomorrow. When moving, whether near or far, you can never tell how long you are going to be disorganised, and what conditions will prevail at the other end. This time is certainly no exception as we don't know where, why or as yet, when we are moving'.

'A strong bitter wind is sweeping through the camp, the sort of day that gives us two alternatives, round the fire or reading in bed. I found no room around the fire, so here I am writing this in bed. Not that I have any bed now as all that was left in India but blankets, below and above, keep you warm even if a little bit uncomfortable'.

Earlier that day I heard about the death of a school contemporary.

I did not find it easy to accept that my turn might come in a matter of hours, days or weeks. The latter years of my boyhood had been spent under the growing shadow of impending war. When it came my generation was snatched away from homes, schools and universities : it interrupted the normal transition from adolescence to manhood. In August later that year I would be celebrating my 21st Birthday. I did not want to die without being given a chance to live. Such thoughts were understandable but it could not have been very consoling for my mother to read, ' I hear Buck Ruxton was killed in Sicily. In the midst of life we are in death—how often do I think of those words when I am told about so and so being killed. Let us hope that this war will really clean up the world—not only Germany, but Britain, USA and everywhere—otherwise these lives have been wasted '.

The move next day began by an uncomfortable train journey to Naples. Inside the carriages were packed reinforcements, all destined to join their units in the 4th Indian Division. Dozens of Italian refugees clung to various parts of the train with many crouching and lying on top of the coaches. We were told they were returning to their homes, or what was left of them, and travelled at their own risk. Several never reached Naples because the steam engine entered a long tunnel, puffing thick black smoke as it laboriously pulled its overladen train slowly behind it. When it emerged, screaming and shouting brought the train to a shuddering halt. Many Italian refugees had suffocated and would never travel again.

It is strange, therefore, that my diary recorded that ' The journey was uneventful '.

Naples for us meant a short night in another transit camp with no time to see anything except nearby Vesuvius which was beginning to smoulder and erupt flames and smoke. Someone told my men that the Germans had dropped bombs into the crater which to the Gurkhas seemed a reasonable act of war. It was impossible to dissuade them. "After all ", they said, "You are always telling us about German atrocities. Why should they refrain from bombing a volcano especially if it's going to disrupt life in Naples ?"

Bomb or no bomb, Vesuvius began erupting in glorious technicolour next morning when we were climbing into the vehicles that were to take us to the southern end of the combat zone, to Venafro. For three nights the glow in the sky above Naples rivalled the dramatic, gigantic fireworks display that was repeated night after night around Cassino, something that we took for granted even if our senses became benumbed.

The recent heavy rain had turned everything into a quagmire, a brown sodden mess. As the trucks moved towards the front line, the countryside became more and more depressing, with American field ambulances and supply units on either side of the road. Our Division was under command of General Mark Clark's Fifth Army, so that everything seemed strange as our trucks, driven at excessive speed by Yankee soldiers, moved towards Venafro. The nearer I got to the front line the less I liked the idea of what I imagined lay ahead. My mother was not given any inkling of doubts or fears : ' Since last writing I have moved up a good few miles through the mud, rain and so on near the Italian battlefields. Not that I have been living in real discomfort as I am at such a distance that a night's rest is assured, and an occasional big gun being the only sign of war, being fought a mile or two over the mountains behind us'.

I have a vivid recollection of a huge railway gun mounted on a mobile platform. In charge was a gigantic Top sergeant, a negro. Flashing a smile at us he shouted : '' Mister Hitler—count your men—fire''—Boom. '' Count 'em again Mister Hitler, fire''—Boom. He, at least, was enjoying his war ! I cannot recollect any lighthearted incident during our stay at Cassino. It was to be a nasty, dirty, grim introduction to war and the passing years have not softened my memories in any respect whatever.

The letter continued : 'Our control in the air is such that I have not yet seen a Jerry plane flying over our district. It certainly makes life easier when you know, automatically, that it is one of ours rather than one of his flying over your head. No mail has arrived but this is to be expected under the circumstances. I hope that some arrives pretty soon when little is happening and I spend day after day waiting until I am wanted forward ; then, no doubt, a lot will be happening'. The next two or three lines were deleted by the censor and even with a magnifying glass years later, they are undecipherable. The letter continued : ' later—I won't tell you when I last had a real bath in the true sense of the word. I realise that I am very lucky to be up here with the chance of joining my battalion any day now'.

The last letter could have done little to cheer my mother up. For her the vigil without regular mail and the bare minimum of news was about to begin. She could but pray that I would survive : her ordeal meant sleepless nights while she waited for a letter to arrive.

Days passed, one week stretched to two, to three, and still there was no news. ' No news is good news' said friends eager to comfort her, but they were aware that there was little that they could do to help.

No letter came because I had not written one. I had tried again and again. But words would not come. When I had time to write and to think, then I did neither : my mind was in a vacuum and I lived for each moment in case it was my last.

Letters there were none but, fortunately, I scribbled in a little brown diary, ' Walker's Diary for 1944 (leap Year)' in which my mother had written, ' Best wishes from Mum'. Lightheartedly I was to write beneath this inscription, " I will need them—all !" Later, in a more sombre vein I added : " This diary to be sent to my mother in the event of anything happening", and signed it Lieutenant E. D. Smith, 7GR, CMF. (Central Mediterranean Force).

Fortunately I retained my diary throughout the war although after April that year, I never used it again. The cryptic short sentences portray little to anyone who did not fight at Cassino in 1944. Many years later, the diary was found in an old trunk. I based articles for regimental journals on the diary and some of those stories now follow.

Thursday, 2 March. " Breakfast—I am going to Div as LO (Liaison Officer). Go there to find mistake—sent after much talk to 11 Brigade past San Michele. Food, quarters fair. Little shelling, Bill Nangle killed by mortar".

What a character Bill Nangle was ! What an ending to a life full of colourful and dashing exploits. As a young subaltern in the Indian Army, in the early thirties, Nangle had spent a riotous few days on leave in Paris. He sobered up to find that he had signed on for service in the Foreign Legion and off he had to go to serve with them in Morocco. He made the best of a bad job, and later, as an NCO, won two decorations for bravery. It was some time before he was able to obtain his discharge—but this only led to his being court-martialled by the Indian Army for desertion. Bill Nangle's career as a soldier, however, was not over. The trouble spot of Palestine beckoned him where he served as an officer in the hard-pressed Palestine Police Force. This episode in his life was brought to an end by the War. Past sins were forgiven and it was not long before Nangle was taking part in raids behind enemy lines, against German installations in the desert, this time as a member of the Long Range Desert Group. And then, finally, the wheel of fortune turned a complete circle when the adventurer became 'respectable' again, by being posted to the Indian Army as an officer in the 7th Gurkha Rifles.

This may conjure up a picture of a dashing flamboyant extrovert but in reality Bill Nangle was quite the opposite. I met Nangle for the first time when we both joined the Battalion in the Lebanon towards the end of 1943. In my twenty year old eyes, the quiet scholarly looking man seemed gentle, unassuming, and old. It was difficult to credit the stories being told about Bill, especially when he sat reading poetry while his younger comrades caroused, drank and sang after the day's training was over. Nangle was from another generation, middle-aged, serious minded, calm in manner and slow to anger. And then, on one occasion only, Christmas Day 1943, he joined the drinkers and the merrymakers and ended up in the small hours of the morning, singing Foreign Legion songs while he demonstrated a whole range of arms drill with a broom handle as his ' rifle'.

In his ' cups' the inner Bill Nangle was revealed to the inebriated British officers and the surprised but amused Gurkha mess orderlies who watched his unrehearsed performance. No one disbelieved the stories any more. Weeks later at Cassino, his company of green, inexperienced soldiers were jittery, ready to run after a long and protracted barrage fired at their position by German ' Nebelwerthers ' and mortars. To calm the young men, the old warrior sat outside his foxhole, puffing contentedly away on his pipe while he cleaned his rifle. A single mortar bomb landed near where he was sitting, and Bill Nangle, who had survived so much, in so many battles, died without a single enemy being in sight.

To make the story more tragic, the company that he was commanding was detached from the 7th Gurkha Rifles under the command of another Gurkha battalion in the division. The CO of the other Battalion was George Nangle : Bill's younger brother.

" Bill Nangle killed by mortar".

Friday, 3 March. " Still destined to be a complete stooge. BM (Brigade Major) explained rough working of brigade HQ—after, nothing to do, very quiet night indeed ".

Saturday, 4 March. " Day passed slowly. Few odd jobs in morning. Rain came on in evening. ' Op Bradman' not before 6th March now. Still bored with life. The nearer I get the more time I seem to spend doing nothing".

The next three days contained similar entries, reflecting boredom and a deep seated fear of being away from the centre of my life at that time, the Battalion in the front line.

And then on March 7, things changed. " BM allowed me to go back to B Echelon to help Duggie. Returned to hear that Tim and I to go up tonight, went back to collect Tim and spend a night at the jeephead. Very quiet".

The next day started : " Waited until shelling stopped before moving off to join Battalion". I was to move up the track to the forward lines but once during my eighteen days as a soldier at Cassino. It was something that I did not wish to do again and the memory of it remained with me for many years afterwards. Before we started walking, I was still like a schoolboy eager to get to grips with the enemy. After all, the war was well into its fifth year and I had yet to see a German soldier. That walk brought me down to earth by destroying romantic notions as our small party trudged up the path towards something so different from what I expected. The track, stony and rocky in most parts changed to slush in the ravines where the incessant rain had turned the mud into a quagmire.

The track was the artery, the jugular vein of the Indian and British soldiers who were crouching in the positions and foxholes on the features tantalisingly near to the Monastery and yet so far from their

final objective. Up and down this track went everyone and everything : from reinforcements still to be blooded, the ration parties
escorting mules on which all kinds of loads were carried, with men
and beasts displaying little keenness to move at speed to the unknown
ahead of them—except when they crossed open areas where the
Germans were mortaring, with their strikes being controlled with
accuracy by spotters on the heights above, in particular on the snow
clad Monte Caira. Then it was a case of a quick prayer and a dash,
with hearts pounding as fast as the legs which scurried to cover the
ground at full speed, spurred on by fear.

New clean soldiers going up, prematurely old bedraggled men
returning.

Down the track came a trickle of men, tired, dishevelled, many of
them wounded, stumbling with the aid of a stick or leaning on the
arm of a comrade, or on occasions being carried with as much care as
was possible over the rocky slopes by stretcher bearers. Few of them
showed any interest in us. Those who were in pain, moved, or were
carried, with one purpose, to reach the bottom of the hill and find
welcome medical care. The utter exhaustion and fatigue that was
written on all their faces was clear to see and discouraged us from
asking questions about our friends who were somewhere in the hills
ahead of us. If the wounded moved slowly, as if they were drugged
sleepwalkers who had witnessed as much as they could take, then the
mule parties going down to the jeephead maintained a fast and furious
pace. Generally speaking the beasts were not carrying anything : they
had delivered their precious loads and their handlers were going to
get to hell out of it as quickly as possible—and who can blame them ?
Many of them had crossed the valley below under darkness and were
short of sleep and, indeed, courage by now. For those who were
toiling up the path, British, Indian and Gurkha, there was no question
of having right of way where the path narrowed and meandered along
by the side of the steep drops. It was a question of survival, of allowing
the trotting muleteers and their animals a free run ; a collision could
have had fatal consequences.

Nothing has been said about the noise because it was almost indescribable, something that could not and cannot be portrayed by
mere words. At Brigade Headquarters I had been indoctrinated to a
certain extent whenever the Allied artillery, behind the battered farmhouse, opened up in anger to send hundreds of shells ' whooshing'
overhead. The sound of other firing, on Monte Cassino and the main
features near it, had been muffled, a background clamour that pro-
claimed that men were at war without intruding unduly on the senses
of an observer several miles away. Now all was changed. Hardly a
moment passed without some noise : it was confusing, bewildering,
as both sides maintained a furious symphony of hate, a cacophony

which blasted eardrums and numbed senses. " Does anyone survive
this, Tim ?'' I asked. Tim shouted : " Many don't and many won't,
I fear''. There was no need to continue with that sort of conversation !

Although I was to walk down the track when the Battalion withdrew at the end of its stint in the front line, Tim Brown was to be
carried down on a stretcher, in pain from a wound which kept him
out of action for several weeks. Tim and I reported our arrival to
Colonel B at advanced Battalion HQ. He was a different man ; a pale
strained face, deep dark circles dark around his eyes ; I was shocked
at the change in our CO.

The diary again. " Sent to A Company, now in reserve. Spent remainder of day in dugout. Good food at 16.30. Bad night, with plenty
of noise''. In a few words this entry described not one day but several
days of our existence near Monte Cassino. Each man's foxhole, his
dugout, became more than a place of refuge, of protection from shell
and mortar, from bitter wind and rain : little holes scraped among
the rocks became precious havens for rest, relaxation, somewhere men
could release their fear without being watched by their comrades,
where they could pray and on occasions live in a dream world where
birds sang rather than mortars crashed and shells screamed above.
With both sides having excellent observation points there was little
movement on the bare hills and mountains during the daylight hours.
As a consequence, British and Germans alike, spent many hours
crouched in their little holes, waiting for the next move, or for the
sudden often uncontrolled bursts of activity which began when darkness came.

After a day or two in the forward positions, the realization that
somewhere and somehow unfriendly eyes were peering at us grew and
grew. Having read books written by Germans, who had been on the
other side of the hill, I now appreciate that they felt exactly the same
as we did. But there were two differences. We had complete air superiority with its obvious advantages. They had their broken battered
shell of an Abbey on Monte Cassino. Whenever we topped the ridge
or put a face out from behind cover, there it was, overlooking us,
seemingly full of unseen enemy, because, invariably, a stream of shells
or mortar bombs would follow. No wonder that the American GIs
cried with joy when about a month before, the building was bombed
by the Allied airforces. The bombardment, in fact, solved nothing :
the Monastery was an excellent vantage point for the Germans, both
for observation and as a last line defence on the summit of Monte
Cassino.

Soon a sort of routine was established by the reserve A Company
which was in a ravine at the foot of the slopes behind the forward
positions. The highlight of each day which remains in my memory
was the arrival of the evening meal and the rum ration. Food was

brought forward as far as possible by mules, thereafter by men carrying hot containers and their precious loads. At times I wondered which was the most important—the food or the rum. I had never touched rum before and disliked the smell and the taste. Its effect, however, on wet dispirited men was quite remarkable ; there was nothing social about our drinking, because we dare not and could not congregate in groups to discuss the day's happenings. It was a question of scuttling back to our dugouts and then, and there, sipping the potent liquor which was like nectar under those conditions. Generous tots of rum, and they were generous when they arrived, diminished fear, eased fatigue, and made it possible to survey the world of desolation around us with some ray of hope in heart and mind. Occasionally the food and the rum did not arrive—or sometimes, the one without the other.

'' Bad night with plenty of noise''. Mention of the noise has been made before, I was to make but one more entry in the diary about it after my first night in the front line. The thunder of the artillery and the crack and whine of the mortars were not bound by the clock, the ugly concert continued by night and day. New sounds that kept me awake during that night in the dugout were caused by the clashes between the opposing patrols and outposts, with the burp-burp of machine guns and the staccato thump of grenades indicating that the static front was alive and full of minor skirmishes. To the reserve company, the sounds appeared to be on their very doorstep, and it was impossible to ignore them. Every now and again, when the firing and shouting of men became louder and louder, I was quite certain that our company would be ordered forward to the assistance of some hard pressed sub-unit. The call for help did not come nor did it ever come during A Company's term as reserve company. However, sleep that first night was an elusive stranger.

Thursday, 9 March. '' Rough toilet. A few shells during the morning. Life not a lot of fun waiting on the receiving end. Sniped before tea''. Not a happy day but, fortunately, it must have ended well, hence the entry, '' Very quiet night''. The problem of washing was not made any easier by the cold weather, not that we had clean clothes to change into anyway. Another worry was to find somewhere conveniently close but not too public for calls of nature. There was a wall over on the other side of the ravine which seemed ideal for my purpose. Unfortunately, there were other occupants of the field as it contained several corpses of dead Americans in varying, despairing postures of death. The cold weather prevented any problems of hygiene but to a young man who had never seen a dead man before, the company of corpses inhibited any desire to carry out a daily natural function. In the end I settled for somewhere nearer my dugout, preferring the gaze of the living Gurkhas to the unseeing eyes of dead Americans.

Similar entries described the next day or two: " Shells before lunch wounded an NCO and two riflemen, enemy sniper continued his work". Then, " weather improving. Day (Saturday, 11 March) fine and warm. What a change ! Ronnie and I sat in the sun reading—whoosh ! ! Shell landed two yards above us. Ronnie slightly wounded —God in Heaven alone knows why both of us escaped so lightly. Am very shaken. With the night rain came—just enough to make foxholes miserable. March 4 remark still applies". (" The nearer I get the more time I spend doing nothing").

I was more than just shaken, I was petrified with fright. After Ronnie had been evacuated to the Regimental Aid Post, I went up to my foxhole and tried to read inside it. To my astonishment I could not hold a book as my hands were shaking violently. The more I tried to concentrate on controlling myself, the more the shivering seemed to spread throughout my body.

" Sahib, you need some rum. Wait, I will bring you some".

This was my cheerful orderly, Rambahadur Limbu, a man with a broad smile and a stout heart. He was younger than I was but seemed to know more about life than I did. A huge mug of rum appeared which Rambahadur said would pull me round. He would not leave until I had taken several sips, choking and spluttering at its potency. Rambahadur urged me to drink more but as it was only mid-day I was afraid that I'd be drunk, incapable of dealing with any crisis that might occur.

Rambahadur had no such inhibitions: " Drink up, drink up Sahib, you need it, you've had a bad shock".

Eventually we came to a compromise and the mug of rum remained in the dugout, still half full, with Rambahadur placated by the promise that I would continue to drink it throughout the afternoon. Later, after darkness fell, the shock returned, and when Rambahadur brought a hot evening meal he found that I could not hold a spoon or the mess tin of rice and stew. He was so worried about his ' Sahib' that he wanted to sleep in the foxhole with me—which would have been uncomfortable for us both. Again, there was a friendly argument and again a compromise was reached: Rambahadur undertook to visit me at regular intervals during the night. Like all Gurkha soldiers he found no difficulty in sleeping under any conditions and in the end, unable to stand the confined space of the foxhole during the long hours of darkness, I wandered over to see and hear Rambahadur and his friend, who were both snoring with innocent gusto. Eventually, towards dawn, I slept and on the morrow the shock had passed : outwardly I was back to normal.

Although back to normal physically the narrow escape had knocked youthful self-confidence out of me. No longer did I entertain boyish dreams of winning decorations at the head of Gurkha soldiers in close combat fighting. I realised that much of war was impersonal, with men being killed and maimed by gun numbers and mortar crews who never knew what damage, death, and destruction they were inflicting on fellow men, their opponents. I cannot recall seeing a single German in daylight during my stay in Cassino : my Battalion did not capture anyone nor did we lose anyone into captivity. Killed and wounded there were many and when we finally withdrew, several were posted as ' missing' but, in the end, they were presumed to have been killed. It was a battle in which no quarter was asked and none given but more casualties were caused by shell and bomb than by bullet and grenade. Cassino taught us that if we were not bored then it was certain that we were being frightened : if we were uplifted for a few minutes by excitement, then the aftermath would be shock which could be delayed. Within us all there was a limited deposit of courage, which could be overtaxed and overspent. Being an officer had one big advantage. The time and effort spent in encouraging the less cour-ageous of our soldiers gave me fewer chances to give way to feelings of fear myself.

Ronnie's relief as company commander was Denis Dougall, himself under twenty-one, but a few months older than I was. Denis returned from a Battalion ' orders' group to announce that the British offen-sive would start when the weather improved. Alas, an hour or two later, on the 12th of March, a Sunday, it rained for an hour at mid-day when I noted, '' Snow on the mountains around Cassino''. The next day was warmer, with the hours passing slowly as the men on both sides waited to see what would happen. '' Spent time reading during the afternoon. Wonder how long this will continue. Quiet night with little rain later''.

Tuesday, 14 March. '' Started very warm but clouded over before lunch. Sniper busy before lunch. Bit colder this afternoon. Chocolate arrived, and had a quiet night''. But unbeknown to us, the long post-poned attack, under codeword ' Bradman', was due to be launched on the following morning. It was to herald the Allies' third major assault against the bastion of Monte Cassino.

Wednesday, 15 March. '' Bradman—08.30 hours. Bombing began and went on until 12.30, a few near our positions. We hear that New Zealanders have captured Cassino. Terrific battle, noise, smoke ; night came after fighter-bombers had continued their work. Artillery fired 1700 shells at night''. A Company had a restricted grandstand view of the fighting on the outskirts of Cassino, being able to see the south-east portion of the much battered town. The bombing, which was directed against the ruined houses and not against the shell of the Abbey on Monte Cassino, was horrifying, even for those who were on the same side as the bomber crews, who rained their destructive loads onto, or near, the German strong-points. When four or five bombs had landed a few yards from A Company's position, no one poked his head out of his foxhole. After a few minutes I felt like shouting that's enough ! but it went on and on until our eardrums were bursting and our senses were befuddled. Some bombs fell on our Company and I found myself shouting curses at the planes. Later I was to write : '' What an inferno is Cassino now. Dear God—take pity on those men, if there are any survivors within the town, which I doubt''.

Later—hours later, it was learned that the New Zealand Division had not managed to capture Cassino. And the tornado of bombs and shells had mutilated and shaken the German defenders but had not destroyed their will to fight. Hence, Thursday, 16 March : '' Learnt that all positions below Monastery have been more or less secured. Jerry very quiet—something coming ? A few enemy shells on our position but no casualties. Attacks at night. We were on a minute's notice throughout the night—no sleep''. Next day : '' Quietish day —reccied paths forward in case of emergency. Sun shining once more. A lot of air activity—what a life !''

Saturday, 18 March : '' Spent last night on patrol without any results''. Nine words that describe hours of conflicting emotions but, in the end, nothing concrete was achieved by my patrol in the battle for Cassino.

It all started with an emergency message to the effect that a strong German patrol had been seen moving below A Company's position. I was told to move down with a platoon to intercept the Germans, to stop them returning with prisoners and vital information. It was my first independent command in action. Moving down the steep hillside in pitch darkness was no easy matter. In my strained ears, I appeared to be making more noise than the twenty-four Gurkhas with me. Perhaps I was as they were like silent cats, undeterred by the rough terrain and indifferent light. We reached the bottom of the hill and took up ambush positions on a much used track which led from Cassino town towards the rear areas of the British positions. Time went slowly and nothing happened. After a whispered consultation with my senior Gurkha rank, a Havildar (sergeant), I decided to send out a small patrol towards a road half a mile away. They set off under the Havildar only to return in haste a few minutes later.

'' Sahib'', whispered the NCO, '' there are some dushmen (enemy) in that quarry, about a hundred yards away. I heard them talking. They don't appear to have any sentries out, I am sure we can shoot them up without too much risk''. In haste we made a plan. A few minutes later, outwardly calm but inwardly excited, I briefed the platoon. Then, it was time to go to the various positions decided on. painfully groping our way over the rocks and stones towards the lip of the quarry. Fortunately, as it transpired, the men had been ordered to await my signal before they opened fire. This precaution saved the lives of several soldiers from New Zealand. The men below, in the quarry, were cooking meals and chattering away—but they were talking in New Zealand English as opposed to guttural German. My Gurkhas were disappointed. At the same time they were scornful about the lack of precautions taken—the complete absence of sentries posted by their New Zealand friends. In silence they moved away from the quarry and as the first rays of dawn tinged the sky, I led them back to A Company. But not to rest.

'' Day came—suddenly had to move down to New Zealand battalion position. Reached there with mule party—a terrible time before arriving at their headquarters. About two-three hours sleep. Rumours of using us in an offensive role''. Dougall had taken the Company down, tactically, while I was ordered to follow with the reserve ammunition, and other accoutrements, loaded on six frightened, noisy mules. Our party did not get very far before an alert German, in an observation post, decided to ' ginger us up' with a few well directed mortar bombs. No one was hit but when the mortaring was over, there were no mulateers—they had fled. The Gurkha escort, of six men, each grabbed a mule and after much coaxing, cursing and cajoling, our tired, angry little party eventually joined up with A Company.

A Company's tribulations were about to begin. The diary tells us : Sunday, 19 March : '' Our Company told to move to attack a point just below Monastery in daylight. Went through Cassino town. God help us. . . '' With little form of warning the Company had to move into and through the rubbled ruins of Cassino, where it was to come under command of the Essex Regiment. Our Company Commander had been told to leave his men near a quarry, on the outskirts of the town, while he went to Brigade HQ for instructions. Half an hour later Denis came back with a long face. Before he passed on instructions to the waiting Gurkha officers, he whispered in English, '' It's the jackpot for us. We are going for the Monastery''. I thought he was joking, but he was not as it became clear when Denis gave out his orders to the astounded Gurkha officers. First of all, the Company was to move up to Castle Hill—a knoll, a promontory above the town but well below the summit of Monte Cassino. On Castle Hill there was a company of The Essex Regiment and A Company was to use their base as a jumping off position for the assault. I was flabbergasted as the implication of Dougall's words sank in. How could any of us survive ? Dougall finished his orders and after the Gurkhas had gone back to brief and collect their respective platoons, told me to cheer up.

With a heavy heart, I replied : ''A master in my school used to say, ' Cheer up lad, you'll soon be dead' and I reckon that sums up our present position''.

We moved into the town. There was no town. It was an indescribable mess of rubble which had been pounded by bombs, shells and mortars for weeks past : truly a ghastly commentary on man's inability to solve problems without resorting to violence. It was difficult picking a way in and around craters, through pools of mud, over collapsed walls of houses. Everywhere there was a pervading smell of death ; of dead corpses, men and mules, a smell that can never be forgotten. Here and there the Sappers had tried to mark out a safe route around a specific area mined by the Germans. On our left, a few hundred yards to the west, we could hear sporadic firing as the New Zealanders and German Paratroopers clashed. Then we came to the edge of the town where we had to cross a valley to the base of Castle Hill, over open ground overlooked by the Monastery above. Once again, we felt that many eyes were gazing down at us from the giant Abbey.

Our Company Commander decided that the three platoons would cross in turn, doubling as fast as possible over the rough ground. The German observers might not be able to stop the first few men but would be ready for those behind. The chance of the men at the rear escaping unscathed was doubtful. Dougall decided that a full five minutes must elapse between the first two platoons and then a further ten minutes before the third and last group began crossing to the base of the hill—and safety. It was a sensible idea except that the unfortunate Smith was told to move as the last man in the last group. Thus I had to witness the others scuttling their way across, watched by friend and foe. Not a shot, not a bomb was fired at the first platoon. The men in the second were not so lucky. Two soldiers were hit by snipers, one being killed outright and the other hobbling his way across. Then followed a long ten minutes as the twenty-five Gurkhas with me waited, continually consulting watches as we all wondered what would happen. The platoon commander, a young Havildar, who had taken over the appointment that morning, began to get excited, saying : '' Let's go, Sahib. The longer we wait, the more likely we are to be hit by everything they've got. It's madness to sit around here''. In my heart I wavered but had served long enough with the Gurkhas to know how to deal with the excited NCO.

'' It is a ' hukum' ; I always thought that Gurkhas obeyed any hukum given by their company commander''.

In Nepali, ' hukum' literally means order but with the Gurkhas' long tradition of soldiering, there is an almost mystical sense about the word, impossible to translate into English. Anyway, my admonition worked on this occasion. And, not surprisingly perhaps, there

was a complete anti-climax when we dashed across without any interference from the enemy whatever. Dougall met us with a broad smile
and ' I told you so'. My reply was that next time I would go with the
first party and he could bring up the rear.

Dougall had received orders that he was to go up to the Castle, on
the top of the hill, and contact the company commander there, to
liaise and having sought his advice, to make a plan for the next phase.
He had been warned that movement up the main track to the Castle
was hazardous because German snipers, from strong points in the
west of the town, were inflicting many casualties. He decided to take a
small wireless with him but not a companion, hoping that he might
slip through where two men would be detected. He told me to get the
men under cover as far as was possible and at the same time, to be
ready to deal with any enemy attack. The senior Gurkha officer, a
Subedar, who in my eyes was an old man but in reality was about
thirty-eight, decided that he would post the sentries : obviously he
felt that I was far too inexperienced for such an important task. Up
to that moment there had been little love lost between us—chiefly
because Dougall tended to use me as his deputy, whereas in normal
circumstances there is only one British officer in a company. The
senior Gurkha officer, a Subedar, is automatically second-in-command. I watched the VCO, Chaturman Rai as he sent off pairs of
riflemen to several vantage points. Then, to my horror, I heard
Chaturman telling a young rifleman to climb up the ledge behind to
the main track which had been under sporadic fire for some time. I
shouted that it would be suicide to send anyone up there. Chaturman
took no notice ; a rifleman clambered up ; there was a crack, a slith-
ering sound and a thud, as his body landed literally at our feet. The
rifleman was dead, with a neat bullet hole through his head. I dared
not speak. There was a red haze of anger over my eyes which made
them prick and well with tears. The dead lad, aged about seventeen,
had been one of the most cheerful, happy-go-lucky riflemen in the
whole Company, full of song and laughter, one who had kept
his friends amused in times of boredom and happy in times of
stress.

I walked away and tried to busy myself with other chores. As I was
gazing at a map, Chaturman sat down beside me, then broke into
tears and sobs : normally a man who stood very much on his dignity
and rarely revealed his feelings to the world, Abir's death had shaken
him badly. It was difficult to find suitable words because in such a
situation there was little to be said. Then the Gurkha officer told me
that Abir was his nephew—they had lived in the same village in East
Nepal ; Abir had been killed before his seventeenth birthday and to
make Chaturman's guilt worse, he had persuaded the recruiting auth-
orities to enrol the lad under age or, more accurately, had told Abir

to falsify his age on enlistment. I was worried that the other men would see the Subedar weeping and so obviously distraught. After thinking out the correct phrases in my rather indifferent Nepali, I spoke to him firmly. '' If you crack, then how can the Company Commander cope ? He is only twenty-one with many burdens to carry''.

Chaturman pulled himself together with an effort, rose to his feet, and in a moment of aberation, saluted as if he was on the drill square, back at the Training Centre in India. He remained a tower of strength until the end of the war ; he and I became the staunchest of friends.

A few minutes later the signaller called out that the Company Commander wished to speak to me on the radio. Dougall's voice sounded cheerful and relaxed. The plans had been changed—for the better, he added. '' The Sunray (commander) here is waiting for confirmation. To save time, you'd better come up here and I will brief you so that certain things can be done before it is dark. Don't bring anyone with you ; move the same way as I did and the best of luck—it's a dicey track''.

I passed on the gist of the message to Chaturman before setting off.

At first the small track running along the side of the hill was well defined and presented no problems. And when I saw the walls of the Castle after rounding the shoulder of the hillside, I wondered why Dougall had bothered to warn me about the shortcomings of the path. My spirits rose as I climbed steadily towards the rear of the position when I saw a wounded British soldier, stumbling his way down the path.

'' How do I get into the Castle ?''

'' No way in from the back—you have to go down and round to the right there. Not that there is any track''.

I followed his directions and came to a point where I had to get across and round a large rock, below which there was a steep drop into the ravine hundreds of feet below. I had a good head for heights and, prior to coming to Italy, had done a basic course in rock climbing. There was a difference, however, because now I was wearing ordinary service boots. When I tried to edge a way round the rock, first one foot, and then the other, slipped until I was holding on for dear life by my finger tips. I did not know whether to try and go back but sensed that if I did, then I would never pluck up courage to reach the Castle by this way. It had to be forward. I moved my right toe over to the tiniest of footholds, braced my body and then threw myself across, clutching at the scree as I fell on the other side of the rock. I slithered a few feet down the slope but was safe. Not for the first or last time that day did I render a sincere prayer to the Almighty for deliverance.

The scene inside the Castle was one of maximum activity, chaos, confusion, of men who defended the walls with desperate courage, and of men huddled behind piles of rubble, some wounded, many worn out and several who had given up completely. It was from this Castle that, in turn, British, Indian and Gurkha soldiers had set out in forlorn attempts to reach key points below the Monastery on the mountain above. A few had managed to reach the isolated body of 9th Gurkhas on a feature called Hangman's Hill but the majority had met with costly rebuffs—and the survivors had trickled back to the comparative safety of Castle Hill. At that particular point of time, on the afternoon of 19 March, there was not much safety for anyone within the walls of the ruined Castle. The German paratroopers had made determined counter attacks earlier that morning when a handful had even tried to scale the walls before being beaten off. Their snipers had inched forward, wormed their way into vantage points, where they made the lot of the defenders dangerous as well as uncomfortable. For the moment, there seemed to be a lull in the battle as if both sides realised that the struggle for Castle Hill was all important but neither Germans nor British had the necessary reserves of strength to win at that juncture.

The commander of the beleaguered castle was a young major, with his arm in a sling, unshaven, exhausted but radiating a calmness and courage that was inspiring those men who were still willing to fight and defend the position. Behind his quiet manner was a fierce determination, it was this strength of purpose that saved us, the men of A Company, 7th Gurkha Rifles. Major Dennis Beckett of the Essex Regiment had seen foray after foray leave Castle Hill only for the survivors to return in dribs and drabs, victims of piecemeal attacks. When Dougall arrived, and asked for advice as to how A Company was to carry out the mission given them by Brigade HQ, Beckett had exploded in anger. He had seen too many costly attacks already, all of which had been ineffective. Moreover he was deeply concerned about the safety of Castle Hill itself : an active fighting company of Gurkhas, near at hand and ready to help his defenders, would be of more use than another broken band of men who, he knew would eventually trickle back like their unfortunate predecessors. He refused to let A Company go forward and told Brigade HQ so in a heated conversation over the wireless. The Brigade Major agreed but as the Brigadier was not at his headquarters, formal permission could not be given until he returned. Denis Dougall explained all this to me, adding that he would have to remain until a decision had been made by Brigade HQ. In the meantime I was to return, to ensure that the platoon commanders carried out local reconnaissances so that if the company had to move forward under darkness, they could lead their men wherever our assistance was required. Denis would come back as soon as the Brigadier confirmed the tentative arrangements. So off I went. ,

Outside, the jagged walls of the Castle looked like a gigantic decayed tooth, with the top whittled away by shell and mortar. I remembered the hair-raising track which had caused so much difficulty on my way up. Surely there must be an easier way ? How could the weary and wounded clamber over the hanging rock face or able bodied men find elusive footholds at night ? So I took the path which went to the right and after a few yards met a group of Indian soldiers who were hiding behind some rocks. Their faces reflected fatigue and fear. ' Dazed with the dust of battle, the din and the cries, the men with the broken heads, the blood running into their eyes'. I greeted them cheerfully, jauntily, but their hearts were heavy.

I asked them the quickest way to reach my company of Gurkhas at the foot of the hill. One huge Sikh replied that there was a short cut behind them but on this they had lost several men from accurate sniper fire. The alternative was the treacherous narrow track I had used before.

" One way you get shot, Sahib, the other you slip to your death. But," he grinned without humour, " if you go that way (pointing to the short cut) you are on your own, we won't move to help you, even if you are hit".

" Why ?", I asked.

" Why ? Why ? The Sahib asks why ? Because we've already lost men doing crazy things for British Sahibs. Now do them yourself". The others nodded in agreement.

I climbed to a boulder from where it was possible to see most of the track as it snaked its way down to the base of the hill. Parts of it were obviously exposed to observers in the west end of the town although I did not know which buildings were still in German hands and which had been captured by the New Zealanders. It seemed as if I would have to cover some fifty yards or more before the track veered to the left where for a short distance, I could find protection from enemy snipers. It was impossible to see what happened after that.

I waited and waited. All was quiet. Nothing moved on the path below. Nothing moved in the town—indeed, there had been little firing down there for some time although the sound of battle behind me, around the Castle, continued as fiercely as ever. I said a prayer, the only prayer I could think of, The Lord's Prayer. Then getting quickly to my feet, charged down the track ; nothing mattered but to get to A Company. It seemed as if I was going to be lucky when, something flicked off my black side-cap as I dived to the ground. I lifted my head and saw the bullet mark. As I dropped so had the bullet missed, but only just, my head. Something had prompted me into diving for cover. In a second I was covered in sweat. Cold sweat.

Everything seemed to stop ; the noise of battle, the guns. Above me a lark was singing clearly and with great zest. Probably less than a minute passed but it seemed an age. A few yards away the Indians chattered on the other side of the hill, they were laughing about the young ' boy Sahib' who refused to take their advice. I longed to call out to them but knew their answer in advance.

I crawled forward and willed myself to make another dash. I prayed with great sincerity, prayed for speed, that the sniper would think that I had been hit already. Into the open zigzagging down the track at the fastest speed I had ever attempted. Once again the crack, crack, a blow on my haversack, and then the safety of another rock. Breathless, in tears and humbled to find that fear had caused my bowels to move, I lay as dead until a glance at my watch spurred me on.

Part of the lower stretch of the track was open but I covered it without any incident. What a relief it was to see the worried face of Subedar Chaturman Rai : '' Saw you come over the top and then fall. We thought you were dead, Sahib. But whatever made you come that way ? The whole world could see you and you are lucky to be here''.

I agreed adding that I would explain later. I had been badly delayed already and it was important that the NCOs were briefed now so that they could carry out their tasks before darkness fell. I began giving out orders, trying to ignore shaking hands and the tell-tale wet patch down my trouser legs.

Half an hour later Denis Dougall returned, having climbed along the side of the hill, risking a fall rather than a bullet. Denis noticed that I was shaken and suggested a short rest would help. I went off to find a reasonably comfortable place under a ledge. A chance to relax but it was not to be. Five minutes later the company runner came up to say that I was wanted by Dougall Sahib. Resignedly I went across to where Denis was talking on the radio to Major Beckett in the Castle. He finished, to turn with a smile and tell me that there was to be no respite. I was to go down as soon as it was dark to Brigade Headquarters, somewhere on the other side of the town, to act as Liaison Officer and possibly return with fresh orders.

'' You had better study the route and try to memorise landmarks now. And take your orderly with you as an escort. I am going to brief the Platoon commanders but you need not listen. Remember the password in case you have to come back into our position at some stage before first light tomorrow''.

It was already getting dark but I was able to locate the approximate position of Brigade Headquarters by using a map and compass. Knowing that Rambahadur, my orderly, had a natural sense of direction, I pointed out our destination to him. We selected the best route and noted recognisable landmarks for the journey we were to begin in about an hour's time. Then Rambahadur brought some tea and a few biscuits which was to be our only meal that day.

When we reached the bottom of the hill it was not long before I realised that the landmarks that appeared to be so prominent in fading daylight, from an observation point on a hill, were not nearly so easy to find in pitch darkness amid shapeless ruins. After about ten minutes I suspected that we were lost. Unfortunately Rambahadur and I could not agree on the direction we should be taking. I had a nasty suspicion that we had gone round in a circle when trying to avoid a mined building which had been marked by the sappers with white tape and a "danger–mines" signboard. Rambahadur had no doubts whatever. He was sure he knew the way. Against my better judgement, I agreed to let the Rifleman lead. The town, or the remains of it, was strangely quiet after a day of close-quarter fighting when the noises of machine guns and grenades had paid testimony to the bitter struggle that was being waged therein. The two of us shuffled and groped an uncertain way around walls, skirting bomb craters, and scrambling over piles of rubble. Occasionally we heard whispered voices or smelt cooking which wafted from out of the darkness, usually from improvised cellars and hiding places. This, of course, explained the lull in the battle because during the daylight hours neither side had been able to cook or even collect water. As I was thinking about such matters, a dark form appeared in front of Rambahadur and challenged him—in German. Before the two of them could recover from a mutual surprise, I fired at the sentry with my tommy-gun, saw him drop, then shouted to Rambahadur to run. We dashed down the remains of an alleyway to throw ourselves behind a wall. The German sentry had fallen—hit by the burst of fire, my first victim in the war. His friends who had been cooking their evening meal below ground, began firing at random, shouting furiously at each other. No one, however, came to look for us and after about five minutes all was quiet.

" We will wait a minute or two and if nothing happens, go that way—and I will lead", I whispered to Rambahadur.

Even in the dark, I could see the white gleam of Rambahadur's smile ; later, after the battle of Cassino was over, my orderly much enjoyed recounting the saga of our journey through the town and how we upset a German section's evening meal.

We set off and after some minutes I recognised one of the landmarks noted from Castle Hill—after that it was plain sailing, with no further incidents, until we reached Brigade HQ. My diary entry was short and simple : ' Went back to Brigade HQ at night. After much discussion, Company withdrew from Castle Hill before morning light'. At the time I did not know what the discussion was about : the Brigadier greeted us courteously with a welcome whisky, and then told us to go and sleep. I drank the whisky, lay down but could not sleep. Rambahadur's snores added to the clamour of battle so a weary officer gave up the struggle. I went back to the improvised Operations room where the Brigadier informed me that A Company would be returning, I was to guide them to a quarry nearby which was to be our temporary position until further orders. It took me quite a time to wake up the reluctant Rambahadur ; together we set out to find the quarry and memorise an easily recognisable route for the Company after they had reached Brigade HQ. In the darkness all this took time and, once more, there was no sleep that night.

A Company had been withdrawn because a German force had begun to infiltrate its way down the large ravine behind Castle Hill, in an attempt to isolate the British garrison by cutting off supplies of food and ammunition. Monday, 20 March's diary entry reads : ' Company in position on quarry. Food for men and rested. Lunch good. Work in evening—one platoon on standing patrol. Heavy and accurate shelling on our position between 3.30 and 4.45. Gerry counter-attacked ' Bowl'. We were rushed up there. Lot of indiscriminate firing by both sides and no sleep ! ''

The next day, 21 March, proved to be just as dangerous, the pressure never relenting for one moment. The short diary entry reveals : ' Shelling of our position in the morning. News came that we were to remain here and mine positions and make proper defences. Went forward to Royal Artillery observation post (OP), feeling very weak, no sleep or food for a long time. No rest at night'.

What the diary did not record was a story which I was to write for my Regiment several years later. After describing the hectic days, I went on to say : '' Soon we were so exhausted that even sleep became impossible. I have never been an efficient ' sleeper' and I was so wound up that I thought that madness was close at hand even if I survived the enemy's fire and bullets. Nature eventually saved me when I was going around the Company's positions after three sleepless days and night. My legs buckled under me, I hit my head and passed out. Gurkha soldiers carried me back thinking I had been killed by a bullet. In the RAP, the Indian doctor who had already supplied sleeping pills without success, soon diagnosed my comatose state. Events did not let me sleep for more than six hours but I was restored to sanity again''.

So it went on, the merciless shelling and mortaring that claimed many victims. A Company was near the end of its tether. The Gurkha soldiers' normal resilient cheerfulness, their toughness, their fatalistic attitude towards life generally, all these admirable qualities that make them such magnificent soldiers had evaporated. I have never seen them at a lower ebb. This was not their kind of soldiering. It provided no opportunities for them to get to close grips with the enemy : for hour after hour they were targets for mortars, shells and the banshee screams of the nebelwerthers. In retrospect I wonder if we could have held on for a further twenty-four hours but, fortunately, events were to save us.

Wednesday, 22 March. ' Shelled when went forward to reccie new positions—this inferno kept up all day—seems only a question of time now. God help us. Heard a rumour that we may be withdrawn soon. Later—we learnt that we were going back to rejoin our own battalion. Night march, arrived very tired'.

Denis Dougall and his Company had been five days on detachment, away from the 7th Gurkhas. It had been five days and nights of tension, of danger, uncertainty and confusion—but chiefly of noise unceasing and unrelenting. I recorded on the following day, ' Recovered a little but still under a strain'. The remainder of the Battalion had been out of the front line but not out of reach of German mortars and artillery. Nevertheless, compared with A Company, the other sub-units were comparatively rested, so that when the 7th Gurkhas moved back into the forward areas once more, the officiating Commanding Officer selected A Company to be in reserve, which meant a return to the same positions occupied a long week before, a lifetime ago. We moved across at night and settled in. Later, Denis and I were sent for by Major Desmond who was acting as Commanding Officer. We were told that the Commander of 5 Brigade had sent a personal message of congratulation commending A Company's conduct when operating in the inferno called Cassino.

'' Who knows but you both might get a decoration'' laughed our officiating Commanding Officer.

The words of praise were enough but Dougall obtained a well earned mention in despatches for his cool courage and inspiring leadership as company commander.

Now to explain how the Battalion found itself being commanded by Major Desmond. In the preface I stated that the story was a personal one and not an official record of the 7th Gurkha Rifles' exploits. during 1944. The self-imposed restriction has been obeyed throughout the book—with this one exception because the background forms part of Colonel B's dramatic departure from Cassino.

I hesitated about including this story but decided to do so because it illustrates so clearly the fickle nature of courage, the insidious infection of open fear—especially when troops, officers and men, are inexperienced and liable to panic when the unexpected happens.

D Company was in a forward position on Snakeshead Ridge, fully exposed to the elements as well as being less than a hundred yards from the nearest German outposts. The conditions were closely akin to those which existed in France during the First World War. Life was tough, there was no relaxation by day or night.

The commander of one of the platoons was a young, intelligent Jemadar. He had obtained promotion at an accelerated rate from Lance Naik up to VCO rank ; his record of service was littered with a series of ' outstanding' gradings earned on military courses. Jemadar Birbahadur Limbu was indeed the ' blue eyed boy' as far as the British officers were concerned ; he spoke excellent English, he was highly thought of, and it was no secret that his name had been submitted for full commissioned rank, which in those days would have meant him transferring to an Indian unit. It is important to realise how high Birbahadur's reputation was in the Battalion because, in a sense, it was to be the prime reason for the downfall of his company commander, and then, Colonel B, himself.

During a night, early in March, the Germans struck at Jemadar Birbahadur's platoon using every weapon at their disposal. For the company commander in his headquarters, a hundred yards or so to the rear, it was a nerve wracking period because no messages came back by runner, wireless or field telephone ; all he heard was a hellish noise, a mixture of shouting, shooting and the crumps of grenades. Like his men the company commander was inexperienced and still had to be blooded under active service conditions. Others were to learn from his mistake ; he was to be the unfortunate man who was suddenly faced with a difficult situation and in the confusion made the wrong decision. From out of the night without any warning came Jemadar Birbahadur Limbu and a handful of Gurkha soldiers. He and they were panic stricken : they gabbled incoherently that the Germans had overrun their position, the ' Dushman' (enemy), had arrived in large numbers and soon would be attacking company headquarters. His story was garbled but it came out quickly. Jemadar Birbahadur was shit scared. And in a few seconds so was everyone else in company headquarters—except for the absent company 2 i/c, Subedar Moke (pronounced Mokey) Limbu who had not returned from a visit to the platoon on the other flank.

It is quite impossible for us to understand what thoughts went through the company commander's mind that night, so many years ago. When we are sitting in comfortable surroundings, well fed and lacking little, sleeping healthily normal hours, it is easy to condemn and throw stones especially when we learn about the outcome of that night ! It is wise to reiterate that Jemadar Birbahadur's reputation was such that few, if any, of the British officers would have doubted his word under those circumstances. It is possible, I agree, that others might have tackled the situation in another way but who can say ? D Company Commander lost his head and after sending a message back to Colonel B, gave the order to the nearest platoon to withdraw and with the frightened men of his own headquarters went back to Battalion headquarters. No contact was made with the platoon on the right flank, which in blissful ignorance sat tight, manning their own defences.

This local withdrawal caused ripples which grew into minor, then major waves of alarm. Colonel B had to report the reverse to Brigade headquarters ; the reserve Battalion, the 4/16 Punjab Regiment, was told to move forward and counter attack D Company's position. At the same time, the news flashed back from headquarter to headquarter, Brigade to Division to Corps. A company position of the 7th Gurkha Rifles had been overrun : were the Germans making a serious counterthrust across the mountains towards 4 Indian Division's supply line ? Did the reverse mean that the Germans had been reinforced ?

The reserve battalion advanced across the ridge line towards D Company's old position only to find Subedar Moke Limbu and a handful of men still in their foxholes, wondering where their Sahib and the other platoon had gone. The much exaggerated German attack, in reality, had been a strong fighting patrol which had 'brassed up' Jemadar Birbahadur Limbu's platoon before returning to their own positions, little realising what had been achieved by the sharp and noisy attack. In the eyes of the military world, it was a disgraceful business, but such things have happened before, especially when 'green' troops have faced their first baptism under fire at close quarters. For the men of D Company it was an episode that they soon forgot, especially when their confidence increased and different commanders convinced them that they were more than a match for their German opponents. But no mercy was shown to the company commander or Jemadar Birbahadur Limbu. Colonel B was in a difficult position because his superiors knew that a company commander had panicked and a platoon commander had been guilty of cowardice ; the company commander, a Scot, was court martialed and lost his commissioned rank ; Jemadar Birbahadur Limbu left the army to return to his village in Nepal, his previously high reputation in tatters. Further punishment was unnecessary for him because in a country where stories of past battles are recounted over and over again, it was certain that Birbahadur could never boast about his exploits in his one and only taste of action.

At the time, we British officers were upset about the punishment meted out to the company commander, especially as Colonel B himself was cracking up before our eyes. We believed that the CO had sacrificed the unfortunate man and our assessment stands up to the test of time. That the company commander was made of sterner stuff than we or Colonel B suspected was to be proved later because he joined a Scots battalion, rose to the rank of Warrant Officer before the war was over, and served with distinction in France. His whole war time career had been changed by the few moments at Cassino when he was influenced and swayed by the panicky funk of a much trusted Gurkha officer. There but for the grace of God went I—and many others, no doubt.

There was an epilogue to that unhappy and unsavoury episode. It was obvious that Colonel B was going to pieces. He was puffing a bit when going up hill—and there were many physical and mental ' hills' around Cassino. The constant noise caused in the main by incessant shelling, began to prey on his nerves until the once cheerful Colonel had become a man near the end of his tether. Afraid, yes, blue with funk, yes again, but it was his sense of duty that kept him going when he was badly scared. He was the only Regular officer in the Battalion —there was no one over twenty-six years of age in the unit who could take over from him. Condemn him as we did at the time, but we were wrong. The Colonel tried to keep going because in his heart he did not believe there was anyone who could command the Battalion under those conditions. Although he was mistaken, let us give him credit for an obstinate sense of duty. His tour as commanding officer came to a sudden end when the Brigade Commander came forward to make an on the spot investigation, following D Company's unfortunate fiasco.

In daylight it was the rule that only two individuals could go from Battalion headquarters to visit the forward company locations on the Snakeshead Ridge. '' Right, let us go and look at D Company's position, before we decide to make any adjustments'', said the Brigadier, a First World War VC, to Colonel B.

'' Right, Sir. Alan, my IO, will take you round ''.

'' No. I want you to come with me'', and the reluctant Colonel B set off with the Brigadier. After they had climbed up the first ridge, the Colonel had to admit to his superior that he did not know the way —although his three forward companies had been in the same positions for well over a fortnight. The Brigadier sacked him on the spot : he found it hard to believe that our commanding officer had not visited his inexperienced officers and men once during their spell in the front line, especially as the fighting on the hills had been reasonably static.

The Adjutant, a war time officer, had to command the Battalion for a few hours until Major Desmond arrived to take over, a twenty-eight year old Irishman, who had been commissioned into our Regiment just before the outbreak of hostilities in 1939. He soon found that there was little wrong with the Battalion other than inexperience and this soon disappeared under the hail of bullets and the crescendo of shells which continued without abatement during our stay at Cassino. But, most important of all, no officer ever allowed himself to be swayed again by panic stricken subordinates. As a later chapter describes, a somewhat similar situation was to occur when I took over Charlie Company on Monte Grillo : with one big difference ; I had a stout hearted Gurkha officer by my side when the crisis occurred, he saved me from making a fool of myself at a time when the margin between courage and fear, victory and defeat, was a slender one indeed.

Unbeknown to us in the Battalion, the generals above had realised that 4th Indian Division was exhausted and would have to be withdrawn. I did not learn of this for two more days by which time I was suffering from a bad stomach. My body, already weak, was crippled by a nasty bout of diarrhoea, a most uncomfortable ailment when the weather was still cold : trips outside my foxhole were purgatory, my body wracked with pain as the Germans added to the misery by shelling enforced movement caused by Nature's incessant calls. Entries on 25 March continue the sad story : ' Bad stomach continued and now very weak—how long can I continue ? Later—heard that 4 Division to be withdrawn tomorrow night. Good news certainly cheered us both up. Advance party from British unit arrived to reccie our positions'.

This was followed on the next day : ' My stomach still very bad. I have to take mules down tonight. Quiet day. Moved off about 10 p.m.—long march and arrived at Portella at 3 a.m.

Again I have to rely on an account written several years later. ''The distance ? Probably less than five miles but for most of the time in the front line the men had hardly walked at all for six weeks. Men were cramped, unfit, mentally exhausted, without any will power. Even though the ordeal was nearly over, the fact did not seem to be understood. The Germans did little to hamper or harass us—indeed, I believe they, too, were relieving their own units but this was not known at the time. All we knew was that our groups of dejected, tired soldiers had to be across the valley before the sun rose next morning—otherwise the whole relief would be jeopardised and we would be sitting targets under the eyes of the German OPs.

'' Never will I forget that nightmare of a march. Officers, British and Gurkha, shouted at, scolded, cajoled and assisted men as they collapsed. At times we had no alternative but to strike soldiers who just gave up ; all interest lost in everything, including any desire to live. By dint of all the measures we could think of most of the battalion reached their transport in time to survive and fight another day''.

The next day I wrote, ' Everyone in high spirits'. I also wrote to my parents. '' Since my last letter, I have attempted at least two, but both were cut short by events, as they say. So, first of all I will thank you for the books. . . . Well, we are back a few miles, resting, cleaning up and eating regular meals once more. Yesterday I took off my clothes for the first time since the beginning of the month ; I slept in a tent, and not in a muddy little foxhole ; and I could not hear the crash and whining of the shells, which I was beginning to think were a part of life up there. It's perfect here''.

" Yes, we have had our first taste of war in that most bitterly contested of places, Cassino. We have learnt a lot by bitter and painful experience, but are far more confident in our ability than before. Inevitably we have had our losses, but these will not deter us, when and if, we are sent back once more . . . . Don't worry, the worst is over and the end is becoming a reality.

Whenever I read the last paragraph, years after it was written, I feel slightly ashamed of the lofty tone I adopted. It sounds like an army commander's ' order of the day' rather than a letter to worried parents. Perhaps I was trying to cheer them up ; certainly I was not to know that Cassino was just the beginning and during the months ahead far worse moments were to follow, both for the battalion and for myself.

Chapter 2

" PATROL-MASTER "

I scribbled entries in my diary for three more weeks, after the Cassino battle was over, then there were blank pages for the rest of 1944 nor have I ever used a diary again. At Venafro I described how the air of euphoria which had held us all in its grip gradually wore off as the realities of life reasserted themselves. The Battalion had to be reorganised, casualties had to be replaced, equipment refurbished, and a host of administrative details put right.

March 28. " Desmond (officiating C.O.) reorganised us today. I am to do Mortar officer. Great shock when old man B turned up. Div Comd visited us after lunch. Seems if we may be off again soon ".

Old man B was the unfortunate Colonel whose health had cracked during the latter stages of the Cassino battle. No one had expected to see him again in Italy. My contemporaries, the younger officers, had no respect for our ex-commanding officer nor were we able to make any allowance for his age or for the original circumstances which had led to him being asked to command the Battalion in action. Colonel B, a veteran of the First World War, had been selected to train a newly raised Battalion and organise it for war ; the intention then was that he would hand it over to the only other regular officer in the unit, his second-in-command. By a quirk of fate, his designated successor was killed by a stray shell when making a familiarization visit to the Fifth Army before the Battalion moved up into the combat zone. At such short notice, there was no one with the necessary experience or seniority to lead the 7th Gurkha Rifles into battle. Colonel B remained in command, little realising that physical and mental strain would soon defeat him because even early middle age was too old for an infantry commanding officer in Italy.

Without any warning he arrived in the mess at Venafro where he was greeted with open hostility. No one knew why he had come. ' How the hell can the old bastard command us when no one has any respect for him ? ' Later Peter, Matt and the other officers were to regret their public display of bad manners, the cruelty of youth with future ideals ahead towards an old soldier whose career had been finished prematurely by events at Cassino, already described.

Colonel B left the mess tent in silence ; it was only then that those assembled realised that he had come to bid farewell, and to wish them good fortune and not to reassume command of the Battalion.

I suspect that the episode left me with a bitter taste because the next day's entry included the remark : ' The spirit isn't the same now'. The camaraderie of the front line evaporated and old tensions and rivalries, likes and dislikes, crept back into Battalion life. Two days later, however, we were to be on the move again. The diary describes the move.

March 31. ' I was ordered to take all wheeled Carriers to Caserta. All arrived safely. All night spent on the railway station'.

Next, April Fool's Day. Loaded with Camerons on first train. Train did not leave until evening. We heard that we are going to Eighth Army Rail head at Foncesia. Arranged to eat with Camerons. Slept quite well in a cattle van'.

April 2. ' Stopped at Termoli where lads had quite a good meal. Arrived at San Vito at nightfall. Unloaded and settled down to another night on a railway station !'

April 3. ' Left at 9.30 for a temporary camp for the Carriers near Terggio. Went off to 8 Division to collect rations etc. We made ourselves comfortable. No news as yet when Battalion due to arrive. Went to REME mess for drinks in evening'.

And so it went on for another two days, waiting around, killing time and having a few impromptu parties in the evenings. ' Had a party in the Officers' Club which ended in most of us returning tight'. The next day I had a badly swollen jaw as well as a nasty hangover. ' Face badly poisoned—I had to take it easy all day. Went to bed early without any food'.

Next day was Good Friday but it was to be a bad day for young Smith who wrote in his diary : ' Face very painful now'. By that time we had heard that the Battalion was due to arrive later in the day before it moved to a location nearer the front line. Although running a high temperature, I dared not report sick fearing that it would be open to misrepresentation just when the Battalion was due to take up operational duties once more. I rested whenever possible but nature won in the end. On Saturday, 8 April I wrote : ' C.O. saw me and sent me off to hospital at once. Face now quite comfortable'.

I remained in hospital for four days, my face improving as a result of a balanced diet and rest. Indeed, I had been thoroughly run down by our experiences at Cassino, by erratic catering, and by a dire lack of sleep. I accepted the enforced sojourn in hospital as being necessary but commented, ' I don't like hospital but it is a change'. The end of that week saw me back with my friends where I was surprised to learn that I had another job—my sole contribution as Mortar officer had been to move by train with the tracked carriers across Italy to the

Adriatic front. The comment was short and to the point : ' I am to be a Battalion Patrol Master. Caught duty officer on my first night back with Battalion !'

The term Battalion Patrol Master is not one used in normal times by the British Army. Certainly I had never heard it before and had to ask Desmond what the appointment entailed. Some background is necessary in explanation. General Alexander, as he was then, had begun switching troops from the Adriatic front to a position south of Cassino ; now the coastal plain was held by less than half the original number of units. Imaginative measures had been taken to deceive the Germans to keep them in the dark about the large scale deployment of forces. Allied deception plans included intensive patrolling across the Adriatic front to simulate normal activity by a larger force as well as to make the Germans apprehensive about the possibility of a limited offensive near the coast. Each battalion had been told to appoint an officer to co-ordinate patrol activities within the unit and to liaise with the battalions on the flanks ; each day there was to be a co-ordinating conference at Brigade Headquarters at which the three unit Patrol Masters would compare notes, share information and ensure that long range patrols did not clash whilst operating in enemy territory.

It was a big job for a young officer and perhaps too big for me. The Colonel, however, could not spare any of his company commanders especially as he was still without the officers who had been wounded during the Cassino battles. Desmond knew little about me except Dougall's report on my activities with A Company during the hectic days and nights we had spent around Castle Hill. He had no doubts about my enthusiasm : he could not be blamed for my exaggerated sense of duty, my sensitivity about delegating dangerous tasks to my subordinates, or my reluctance in sending men out without accompanying them myself. The Patrol Master's functions should have been detailed planning before briefing his subordinates, as well as co-ordinating all the unit patrol activities ; only on special occasions should it have been necessary for the Patrol Master to have sallied forth himself.

We are, perhaps, anticipating events a little but in retrospect the period I spent as Battalion Patrol Master did rekindle romantic notions and ideas about war which caused me to overtax myself.

On Saturday, 15 April I went with the Commanding Officer to B Echelon where the four rifle companies were concentrated, prior to moving up to their respective battle positions. To my delighted surprise I was allowed to select men from those who had volunteered to join the Patrol platoon, twenty-five hand picked men who were prepared to undertake the more hazardous of the long range missions behind the German lines. There was no shortage of volunteers. The problem was to decide who could withstand the nervous tension of regular patrols, all of which would demand endurance, fortitude and quick thinking in emergencies, planned and unplanned. On my own I could never have selected the right men because my experience with Gurkhas was limited but two senior Gurkha officers (VCO's) were there to advise and, in the end, they produced a tough smiling group of junior NCO's and riflemen, ready to follow me anywhere. The Patrol platoon was kept in being for about six weeks and with one exception, the men selected by the Gurkha officers were excellent soldiers in all respects. Truly it was a small corps d'elite.

There remain but two more entries in my diary and then, probably because of the patrol activities, I never wrote in it again.

Sunday, 16 April entry was as follows : ' Closed Patrol platoon during morning. Remainder of British officers went on reconnaissance of new possitions. I went once more to B Echelon and by end of day had collected most of my men '.

Next day, ' Our General visited the Battalion during the morning. Went to B Company and selected three further volunteers. Sent in my first patrol report. Battalion to take up operational positions and locations tomorrow'.

So much for the diary. Regrettably, too, there were to be no letters to my parents for nearly two months so I have to rely on an account written for my Regiment shortly after the War was over.

Our Battalion moved up into the forward area near the market town of Lanciano. In the full flush of spring the weather was beautiful with the countryside gentle, undulating hills and valleys, such a welcome contrast to the rugged, harsh mountains around Cassino. In the small towns and hamlets there were many scars of the conflict, buildings had been destroyed, the pockmark of shell craters disfigured parts of the countryside especially near the main roads. The larger villages within range of artillery and mortars were uninhabited because these were subjected to regular doses of shelling and mortaring by both sides. The battalions and companies, however, tended to accept the risk of using isolated farmhouses either as headquarters or observation points. In years gone by, the Italians had been in the habit of building villages on the crests of hills and ridges ; observers and snipers now used these excellent vantage points, accepting the obvious danger of being inside buildings which could be seen by the enemy.

The tempo of war was much slower than the Battalion had experienced at Cassino : there was not the incessant unrelenting noise nor did battles flare up each day and every night. Nevertheless, the Germans, like the British, worked their few units hard because they, too, had ' thinned out' : recognising that an Allied attack was inevitable on the main front, they had moved formations across to help their comrades foil General Alexander's spring offensive. The German 334 Division had been operating near the Adriatic for some time and consequently it knew the area well. It had a distinct advantage over us, the newly arrived 4th Indian Division, especially in the art of patrolling : local knowledge of the most likely approach routes was invaluable when scattering lethal ' schu' mines which were to inflict many casualties on their opponents, striking fear in the hearts of our British, Indian and Gurkha soldiers as they moved slowly through the night.

So much for the background. After concentrating all my men into a platoon, we had a comparatively easy two weeks during which four short reconnaissance patrols were carried out to familiarise ourselves with the countryside. I selected routes and tasks which entailed an ever increasing degree of skill by the patrols in order to build up confidence, and as far as I could forecast, without risking a definite encounter with the Germans.

The keenness and enthusiasm of the members of my platoon was exhilarating and made the task of training them an easy one. Each of the four NCO's was given a patrol mission which he had to carry out under my supervision but without any other assistance from me, his officer. I moved with each of these patrols to obey the leader's instructions in the same way as the other members of the party did. At least that was the theory of the matter but on each occasion at the first halt, the Naik or L/Naik (Corporal/Lance Corporal) came back to seek advice or report his next intention. He was to met by an angry whispered reply : '' I am Rifleman Smith. You are the commander : I gave you the mission—carry it out''. It was not easy for the young Gurkha NCO's to pretend they were in charge when there was a British officer a few yards behind, following them. Nevertheless, as they had been selected for their initiative, they took the point and did not dare repeat the error. These test patrols finished satisfactorily, I was proud of my men. We held a small celebration party when rum flowed freely, madals (drums) beat frenziedly while the Gurkhas sang and danced with gay abandon until the small hours of the morning. Most of them spent the next day feeling sorry for themselves. Then it was to be the real business, long-range patrolling behind the German lines.

Our patrols carried out during the first week moved considerable distances but kept well away from known German strongpoints while they probed behind and between the enemy defences. These reconnaissances had no aggressive intent although each patrol had to be capable of looking after itself in any emergency—as far as this was possible.

Inevitably, there were large gaps between the German sub-units because like the British, they were trying to defend a wide stretch of country with comparatively few troops. It was not difficult for a handful of men to get behind the German lines although it was not always easy to avoid detection. The enemy sent out static patrols to listen, watch and ward, located near the obvious approach routes ; by using radio or field telephones they were ready to bring down pre-registered fire by mortars and artillery on to anything suspicious seen or heard near their hiding place. Lavish use was also made of ' schu' mines, a small but deadly weapon of war. These were strewn with ingenuity by the Germans at known crossing places in the hedges, or at fording points in the streams and rivers, or on tracks likely to be used by Allied patrols at night.

The members of the platoon accepted that there would be mines but when the early patrols returned without mishap, gradually learnt to disregard them. Then the inevitable happened. Six men had completed their mission without any incident and were expecting to be challenged by a C Company sentry when they were within a hundred yards of an outpost. Suddenly there was a sharp explosion, following which the leading scout, a rifleman, collapsed with a shattered right leg.

He survived but his leg had to be amputated below the knee. In any society such an injury would have been a crippling blow ; for the Gurkhas of Nepal it was and is a tragedy beyond words as most of them earn a living as subsistence farmers, working hard for little reward in a land of much beauty, where life can be cruel and tough, especially for the old, the sick, the maimed and the disabled. Loss of a leg or an arm deprives a man of his livelihood and for the simple people who dwell in mountain villages, there is no ' welfare state'.

Not unnaturally the wounded riflleman's plight had a profound effect on the morale of the other members of my platoon. The next day there was no rush to volunteer ; the men had lost their normal cheery, confident smiles. I was worried and went to consult my Colonel. Together we discussed the tasks that had been given to the Battalion by Brigade Headquarters before we selected the easist one. Desmond agreed with my suggestion that I should lead the next patrol which, I felt, should go out that very night.

' Yes, Birdie, I agree because they will only brood about it. Better get it over and done with. It's rather like being thrown off a horse— the longer you wait the less chance there is that you'll ever climb on the damned beast again'.

It transpired that the patrol passed without any major incident and was duly recorded in the daily ' situation report' as N T R (nothing to report). It is true that no Germans were seen at close quarters during the seven hours spent away from the friendly security of our Battalion. Nothing spectacular was hidden by the official report though there was enough nervous tension for me, the officer, and my six men as we moved off from D Company's position at 8 o'clock in the evening. At first it was a darker night than usual so that the members of the patrol had to move within a pace or two of each other. Two riflemen went ahead with me a yard or two behind them. After we left D Company's location, all was quiet with nothing to indicate that anyone was at war. The silence was unearthly as if both sides had decided to have a night's rest, a night of peace. It was as if we were on a training patrol ; it was hard to realise that one of us might be killed or maimed by bullets instead of play acting at the sound of blank ammunition : any bullets that night would bite as well as bark. And no mines, I hoped, and regretted that I had challenged fate by being so optimistic.

As if to emphasize this point, the leading scout gave a halt sign with his right hand. Like well trained circus animals the other men of the patrol immediately took up positions, facing outwards in different directions, so that they could guard against a surprise attack from any quarter. They lay on the ground with eyes and ears straining to pierce the dark silence around them. Nothing moved, nothing stirred. Above us clouds scampered rapidly across the sky, sometimes covering and then revealing a half strength moon ; at times we could see quite clearly and then suddenly it was as black as pitch. The intermittent rays of light helped us to maintain the correct direction but at the same time we could expose our movements if we ever became complacent and careless.

I whispered to the NCO beside my side, L-Naik Aitaraj Limbu, '' we must freeze for a few seconds each and every time the moon appears, only taking up positions if anyone is suspicious''. The gist of these instructions were passed from man to man before I gave the signal to move : each man rose with deliberate caution taking care not to make any noise by stepping on a twig or knocking a stone.

Off we went, reacting to the moon as it flashed on and off. It was a slow business, too slow as the minutes ticked by and our objective, the farmhouse on the hill opposite, seemed to be as far away as ever. I peered at the luminous hands of my watch and did not like what I saw. Obviously more speed was essential but at the same time I was anxious to avoid a rash noisy approach.

I consulted Aitaraj, an intelligent young man, who was never afraid to give his opinion or voice suggestions to his superiors. There was a close bond between us which transcended differences in rank, race, religion and—something considered irrelevant in the Gurkha Brigade—colour. Aitaraj was the most junior of four NCO's in the platoon which allowed me the chance to select him as my deputy whenever possible. My faith and trust in Aitaraj was implicit and I sensed that my feelings were reciprocated by the NCO. We were friends who respected the artificial conventions imposed upon us by rank but were close to each other in bonds of affection and comradeship.

Aitaraj suggested that only three members of the patrol should go to investigate the farmhouse. Although the building seemed to have been left unoccupied in the middle of No Man's Land- Brigade Headquarters suspected that the Germans were using it, at irregular intervals, as an observation post. The rest of the patrol, the NCO suggested, should move to the right flank where, on a prearranged Verey light signal, they could open up with covering fire should the reconnaissance element run into trouble. It seemed sensible.

Who was to lead it ? At once Aitaraj volunteered to take the two best riflemen with him but I could not accept that suggestion. I hated the idea of sending others into danger whilst I watched at a distance in comparative safety. The L/Naik's argument that the Sahib's height and pale face would make him far more conspicuous than three stocky, dark complexioned Gurkhas was a difficult one to refute. An older, more experienced officer might have given in gracefully without further ado. I did not and could not. My mind was made up. I would go with two others. As time was short, further discussion was pointless. Aitaraj gave in on one condition—he insisted on accompanying us. It meant leaving the ' covering party' under the command of a rifleman which if things went wrong might be an unacceptable risk. Nevertheless all the riflemen in the platoon were potential NCO's ; the risk was worth taking because Aitaraj's skill, like a silent poacher in the darkness, was without equal in the battalion—in my opinion anyway.

The three of us set off, Aitaraj in the lead, then me, with the riflemen, Ramsing Rai, in the rear. I decided to let the NCO select his own route ; Ramsing and I followed Aitaraj's instructions and hand signals without any hesitation. Aitaraj's instinctive use of the ground was ingrained in him, the hunter who had learnt his skills as a child in the hills of Nepal. ' To think that I had the temerity to put this chap through my training programme', I thought, ' he knows more about it than I will ever do, even if I live to be a hundred '.

By now we were approaching the river in the valley below and it was here that extra precautions had to be taken as crossing places would be under surveillance or mined or both. There had been heavy rain earlier that day which would have raised the level of the water although, previously, patrols from the Battalion had crossed with ease, the water being below knee level. We would be vulnerable while crossing especially if the moon was shining ; on the other hand if we tried to cross in complete darkness there was the likelihood that we would make more noise, stumbling and groping our way across to the other bank. When carrying out a personal postmortem later, I realised I should have brought our protection party closer into positions where they could have given intimate fire support while we crossed the river. By now the others were moving towards higher ground on the right from where they could fire at the farmhouse : unfortunately they would not be able to see the stretch of river which lay below the three of us.

Three pairs of eyes searched for signs of enemy movement and tried to judge how deep the river might be. The recent wounding of their friend had made a strong impression on the two Gurkhas so they did not want to cross where the river was easily and obviously fordable. There would be mines, they said. I asked if they could swim and the answer came, ' No '. As they hail from a land-locked country, few Gurkha soldiers can swim until they are taught to do so after enlistment. Unfortunately in the Second World War, there was not the time or opportunities to carry out such training. ' Good God', I thought, ' three non-swimmers' because I had never conquered a deep seated fear of water and drowning.

' Let's hope it is not too deep ; that bend over there seems to be hidden on both banks by thick undergrowth. We will cross when the moon is out. It will make it easier and we will go one at a time. I will go first''.

'' No, you won't, Sahib'' whispered Aitaraj, '' I've crossed many more rivers than you have in my own country, far deeper than this. Let's stick to the order we are in now''. Ramsing nodded in agreement so there was no point in arguing any more.

It took considerable patience and a degree of agility to move down the steep bank through a scrub of thickets and thorns. In my ears, we appeared to be making a terrible noise but the muttering of the river below was probably louder, especially for those listeners on the other side of the valley. We reached the water's edge with scratched hands and faces, and clothing badly torn by the undergrowth. Ramsing and I took up positions ready to fire across at the other bank while Aitaraj began to examine the fast flowing river, using a stick to judge its depth in order to select the easiest fording place. At last he was satisfied and gave a thumbs-up signal before setting off. The water was well above his knees. Then it was my turn. Being taller than Aitaraj, I should have found it easier but without his wonderful sense of balance, stumbled and nearly fell as I was nearing the other side. Ramsing crossed with disdainful ease. We went to ground for a few minutes to check whether our crossing had caused any visible or audible reaction by the enemy. There was not a sound ; indeed the whole front continued to be shrouded in peaceful silence. We were getting cold as a result of wet feet and clothing. The farmhouse was less than three hundred yards above our heads with a gentle approach after we had clambered up and through some more undergrowth.

How were we going to discover if there were Germans in the building, especially if the enemy sentries were hidden behind cover and made no noise ? A plan had been rehearsed earlier in the afternoon which had involved all seven members of my patrol. Now something different was required : it had to be quick, it had to be simple, and it had to avoid any fighting if at all possible.

My idea was that one of us, preferably Aitaraj because he moved like a silent panther, should get to within throwing distance of the house from the left, while the other two moved, at a safe distance from the house, to the right flank. Aitaraj would then throw a stone which, I hoped, would provoke some sort of reaction from the men inside the building—if there were any. Should the Germans pin-point Aitaraj's position and open fire at him, then I would release a green Verey light—the signal for the other members of the patrol to render support as a diversionary measure. Ramsing and I would observe and listen before withdrawing to the crossing point as quickly as possible, where we would meet up with Aitaraj. The two Gurkhas seemed satisfied with the plan, it was well after midnight and no more time could be wasted in discussion anyway.

After we emerged from the undergrowth, it was time to part company. The farm building was already visible and as Ramsing and I moved closer the tension made me feel like an overstretched piece of elastic. When we were less than a hundred yards from the house, the two of us crawled towards a low broken wall from where we could watch and listen. The sky had become increasingly cloudy with the moon a rare and fleeting visitor, niggardly with its rays. While the indifferent light would help Aitaraj in his task it would make it difficult for us to see any movement after the NCO had hurled a stone at the building. Much depended on the nerves and self discipline of the Germans, assuming that they were there. How would they react to the sudden noise ? I hoped that they would begin firing and thus not only disclose their presence but also give an indication of their numbers and the weapons they were carrying.

As we reached the wall I had a sudden unnerving fear that there might be some ' Schu' mines strewn around by the occupants of the farm, in order to protect themselves from any intruders. Like a fool I warned Ramsing : inch by inch we groped our way towards the best vantage point, while I cursed myself for having developed nerves at such a crucial stage. By now Ramsing was paralysed by the same inhibitions ; naked fear is infectious and can strike others without any words being spoken. Nothing exploded, however, except in the imaginations of two frightened men.

We listened for several minutes ; the only noise we could hear was the muffled murmur of the river as it bubbled its hurried way in the valley below. Where the hell was Aitaraj ? Had he also become apprehensive about mines ? How much longer could we wait ? All these and other thoughts went through my mind as with nerves taut and jangling we maintained a silent vigil.

When something did happen it came as a complete anti-climax.

From just outside the door of the house came a distant cough then the subdued murmur of voices.

Ramsing whispered, " Dushman" (enemy), then tucked his rifle into his shoulder.

" Don't shoot, you fool : we are not meant to be killing them tonight". The Rifleman relaxed but kept his rifle in the ready position just in case.

" What do you think Aitaraj is doing, Ramu ?"

" I bet he is on his way back to our RV. He will have heard the dushman surely".

It seemed the most likely explanation but unbeknown to us Aitaraj, being on the other side of the building, had not heard the cough. He threw his stone at the same time as we were beginning to move back from the cover of the wall. We heard it land and froze in our steps, not daring to stir a muscle. Someone challenged in German, then all was silence. We waited and waited but nothing more was heard. No one fired, no more voices were raised. The enemy's self discipline had stopped any indiscriminate firing but had not been strong enough to stifle the sentry's challenge when startled by the stone that had landed near him, out of the dark night. Back to the river we went, resisting as best we could a strong urge to run or at least hurry away from danger. It was not easy to do this but it was important that we were as quiet and alert coming back as it was when going out on a mission. In time, some members of the platoon were to learn such a lesson when, returning at full speed they were ambushed barely two hundred yards away from a Battalion outpost. In the small hours of the morning 27 April, such a mistake was not made although every nerve in our bodies was crying out for more speed.

For a few minutes there was no sign of Aitaraj at the crossing point until he announced his presence by a faintly spoken pass word from the other side of the river to where we were waiting. Ramsing and I forded the river without mishap to join him.

" I saw three Dushman, Sahib, after I had thrown the stone. They came out of the building and took up fire positions".

" Did they see you ?"

" No—if they had, would I be here ?"

" Maybe not—let's talk later ; it's nearly 0400 hours and the others will be on their way back to D Company. Ramsing—you lead and move slowly".

We maintained and observed all the normal precautions, stopping

every few yards, taking up positions to watch and listen. I can remember thinking, a model patrol, then feeling guilty once more
because each time I challenged fortune something always seemed to
happen. It did—again. When we were crossing an open field there
was a fluttering whistling noise of bullets flying just above our heads.
We threw ourselves to the ground. The chattering of heavy machine
guns kept up the fire which fortunately passed within a few feet above
us as we lay flat on our faces. It was impossible to say whether we had
been seen or whether the Germans had their machine guns firing on
fixed lines and had opened up just in case. At least, that was my first
thought but a few minutes later down came some mortar bombs.
Now there was no doubt whatever : we had been seen on our way
back by a German patrol which had reported our location with
accuracy. There was nothing we could do but hug the earth and hope
for the best. Recent rain had made the ground soft and this nullified
splintering and ricochets to a great extent—and saved our lives.
Nevertheless three shaken and bedraggled men rose after it was all
over to move faster than they had done before, towards the safety of
D Company nearby. There we found the whole Company manning
defences, not sure whether an enemy attack was impending. Ramsing
gave the pass word in a bold voice as he was afraid that a jittery,
trigger-happy sentry might fire first and ask questions afterwards. As
he explained to me later, he never trusted D Company anyway—his
own friends in Baker Company had forgotten more about soldiering
than D had ever learnt !

At D Company headquarters, we greeted the other members of the
patrol who had spent an uneventful and boring night—they grumbled.
It was a wonderful feeling to be back among friends, to drink a mug
of steaming tea with generous helpings of sugar. I reported by field
telephone to Desmond who told me that I would have to go back to
Brigade Headquarters to be debriefed. No rest for me today, I thought
ruefully, as the men went off to their billets and then to sleep. Never-
the less I was pleased with their performance. While I tried to keep
awake during the jeep journey to Brigade Headquarters I was happy
to think that it was the last time we might have to visit that farmhouse.

If it had been then it would have been quite certain that I would
not have remembered so many details of the patrol just described.
Little did I know that it was to be but the first of three visits and the
least eventful of them all.

At Brigade Headquarters I was interrogated at some length by the
Intelligence officer. He explained that the Brigadier had a bee in his
bonnet about that ' damned house'. Evidently it had been given a
code name, Windsor Castle. He went on to say :

" The old man is convinced that the Gerries are using it and, on occasions, leaving observers there throughout the day. As a result the bastards have a damned good view behind the 4/6 Rajrif and your left hand company position''.

I did not disagree but asked him what the next step was, with some foreboding.

'' I'll let him tell you himself. Anyway he asked me to say how well you had done. Go and get some sleep and tomorrow after the co-ordinating conference, the Brig is going to talk to you for a few moments''.

On the way back sitting next to the driver in the jeep, I fought to keep awake and indeed once bumped my head on the windscreen in front. The driver grinned in sympathy.

'' Don't worry, Sahib, you'll be able to sleep all day and night when I get you back to our lines''.

'' I hope so'', but already my mind was going round and round, wondering what the implications of the Intelligence officer's remarks were for my patrol platoon. Only the morrow would tell.

Sleep was a long time coming. Work by day, sleep by night, had always been my way of living and it was not easy to change a habit of a lifetime, desperately tired though I was. I felt excited and elated as if I had been drinking champagne on an empty stomach. After trying to rest in the afternoon, I went to the small improvised mess that was used by our Battalion Headquarters' officers. I wanted to unburden myself, to talk about the patrol but was chary about doing so in case others were not interested or accused me of being big-headed. Topics of conversation which interested every member of the mess were never easy to find. For example, the doctor could and did produce many gruesome stories which usually ended with his listeners telling him to ' shut up, Doc'. Women were a safe topic although in that particular area there were none near the front line. The Adjutant was a well practised Lothario, not averse to regaling his listeners with stories of his conquests which included maidens in Cairo, Beirut and, more recently, Naples. That night found the conversation more trivial than usual and after a couple of drinks, I returned to my bed—to sleep but fitfully. Next day I went to see the Brigadier.

To a subaltern of twenty any Brigadier seemed like a person from another world—indeed I had only ever spoken to one just before I had graduated at an officers' training school in India. The Brigadier I met on 28 April had a distinguished war record as a commanding officer in the Parachute Brigade and had recently been promoted. He was a thin wiry man who radiated great energy and exuded self confidence. Unfortunately someone had once told him that he was like General Bernard Montgomery and consciously or unconsciously, Brigadier Hawke had modelled himself on the great man. I liked him but I knew Desmond and the other commanding officers in the

Brigade had distinct reservations. Hawke had big ideas and plenty of dash, ideal for the fluid, open warfare of the desert but now sadly held in fetters by the difficult Italian terrain with its mountains, blown bridges and mine fields, all of which assisted tenacious German defenders. Hawke drove his Brigade hard and not always with happy results.

Three months later he was killed in an aircraft crash.

The Brigadier got down to business without any preliminaries. Our conversation went something on these lines.

"I don't think that the Germans use Windsor Castle as a permanent post, do you Smith?"

Me: "I don't honestly know, Sir. I agree that it would be a bit isolated for them as well as dangerous if they sat there all the time".

"That's what I think, Smith. I also believe that if we got someone into the top rooms of the building, they would have a damn good view over to the left, over the German's positions there", and he showed where he meant on the air photographs on the table before us.

He went on to explain that his idea was that two or three men should go to Windsor Castle and stay there for twenty-four hours, being in direct touch with artillery and mortars so that if big targets presented themselves during the daylight hours, these could be shot up. Evidently, an Italian agent had reported that Windsor Castle was used by the Germans every four or five days: it was thought that they realised that too frequent use of the excellent observation post would lead to it being a popular target for Allied artillery and even shelling by tanks. If intelligence was correct, the Germans would not be using the house for at least three days. Hawke wanted me to go there as soon as possible, preferably that night, but if time did not permit, then definitely during the following night. I was to remain there for a whole day to record enemy movements seen and, if any targets presented themselves, from our observation post in the house to direct and control our guns and mortars. This meant, of course, taking a small wireless with us.

I asked one question. "What do you want me to do if I find Gerry is already in the house and he doesn't show any sign of moving out, Sir?"

"Use your discretion, Smith, but if there is no sign of him moving by 0400 hours, then you must come back. In such a case we can then plaster the house during the day", replied the Brigadier. "I am certain you will find the house empty. This Eytie agent is usually accurate, he reckons we have got it to ourselves for two or three days. Once you come back, we can consider whether we should knock the place down. On the other hand it could be of more use to us than it is to him because I am sure you are going to get a clear view across that valley there"—pointing to a valley on the air photographs.

At this stage he was called away to speak on the telephone to the General. The Brigadier had suggested that the fewer men that went the better although he agreed that it might be wise if a protection patrol escorted my party out to the house and then, on the following night, shepherded us back and into the battalion forward locations.

It was too late to arrange such an enterprise that evening even though Brigadier Hawke had indicated, with his normal impatience, that he wanted 'action today'. I decided that two companions would be enough especially as we had to sit during daylight hours in a small, cramped room upstairs. One of the men would have to be a trained, reliable signaller who would have to combine the qualities of courage and fortitude with high technical skill as a radio operator. After reaching Battalion Headquarters I sought out the Signals officer and asked him for advice. He told me that the best chap was already in my platoon. He had hated losing him to a rifle company but the NCO had insisted that he wanted a more exciting life and, as a consequence, left the signal platoon when the Battalion arrived in Italy. I asked him who this chap was. He replied : "A guy called Aitaraj Limbu". I felt ashamed that I knew so little about the background of my own men, especially trusted Aitaraj. In fact, it was not so surprising when it is remembered that these men came from all companies in the Battalion while I had only rejoined the unit during early March of that year. Anyhow, one important problem had been resolved.

I sent for Aitaraj and told him what was in store for us. His only worry was that he was being asked to be a signaller again. He made me promise that when the patrol platoon was disbanded he would go back to his rifle company rather than to the signal platoon. The promise was duly given.

" Shall we take Ramsing with us ? We both know he is tough and reliable," I asked.

" Ramsing is good but your orderly Rambahadur would be better. He's not so intelligent but he won't flap whatever happens."

We agreed to think about it and to compare notes in the morning. In the meantime I selected and gave a warning order to the escort party which was to consist of Lance Naik Bilbahadur Tamang and five riflemen. In a small body of men news travels fast. Later in the evening Rambahadur brought me my evening meal of curry and rice. Nothing was said about the operation until the meal was over. Rambahadur cleared the table and then stood rigidly to attention.

" Sahib, I have one point. What time do we go out tomorrow night ? Do you want me to take a tommy gun or a rifle ?"

" Who the hell said that you were going, Ramu, you so-and so ?" I snorted half in irritation and half in jest.

" Ustad said that I would probably be going. My job is to protect you, Sahib. The Subedar-Major Sahib gave me a hukum to that effect''.

I told him that Aitaraj was not commanding the platoon and that I would make the decision.

Rambahadur again stood to attention and said yes, he knew. And he busied himself with various tasks around the room, tidying things up, giving a loud tut-tut at the sight of a pair of particularly muddy shoes, and generally making it clear by his attitude that he was in no hurry to leave until his officer gave in. The battle of wills continued because I could be obstinate when suspicious of being pressurised into a certain action. Eventually Rambahadur could think of no more excuses and, again, clicked his heels together.

'' I have finished everything, Sahib. Shall I attend the briefing with the patrol tomorrow ?''

I could not help laughing and admitted defeat, adding that he would be for the high jump if anything happened to me.

The next morning those men that had been selected to go on the patrol gathered around a sand model which the Intelligence section had prepared from maps and air photographs. It showed the Windsor Castle farm and its immediate surroundings, including all the main landmarks. With our recently acquired knowledge, I had been able to add one or two details until it seemed to give a reasonably accurate picture of what lay before us that night.

I urged my Gurkhas, the two NCOs and six riflemen, to speak their minds and make any suggestions. Soon our first major decision was taken. We would approach Windsor Castle from a different direction even if it meant, as it did, a longer approach march. This would see us leaving from A Company's forward locations on the left of the Battalion sector rather than the centre as happened last time. Assuming that the house was empty and after three of us were safely ensconced in the top room, the escort party would return by a different route to the centre company's outposts. Many other points were discussed and finalised so that after about half an hour, each man knew all about the routes to be taken during the inward and outward journeys, the formations to be adopted, passwords, Verey light signals and emergency drills.

The men left to prepare themselves and to rest whilst Aitaraj and I co-ordinated the communications aspect of the small operation. A signaller in Battalion headquarters would remain on ' listening watch' at all times, ready to pick up any message that might be transmitted by Aitaraj. As there might be occasions when it would be dangerous to use the radio, the initiative would remain with us : we would call up Battalion headquarters whenever circumstances permitted and when there were important messages to pass to the Colonel. Aitaraj went off to fix up minor details with his friends in the signal platoon while I had a final discussion with Alan Howard, the Intelligence officer.

Alan, a Geordie, did not share the Brigadier's optimism about the potential value to us of Windsor Castle as an observation post. He could see why the Germans used it occasionally but failed to understand why a Battalion patrol should be risked on such a venture. Jokingly he advised me to take some playing cards because a whole day, spent in a small room, would be extremely boring—in his opinion anyway. Desmond did not make any comment except a quick 'don't do anything rash and don't stay out there if the bloody Hun is knocking around the house'. On this a promise was easily given !

Just before dark I inspected the members of my patrol with meticulous care to make certain that no one carried any item that could identify him in the event of capture by the enemy. Of greater importance I checked that there were no squeaks and rattles in our equipment and clothing. All seemed to be in order including Aitaraj's radio which had been netted in with the control wireless in Battalion headquarters.

The journey out to Windsor Castle went without incident. It did not take as long as we had expected, chiefly because the level of the water in the river had dropped considerably, so that our crossing was a simple ' paddle'. We moved slowly up towards the house where our escort took up the positions they had rehearsed before coming out on patrol. Meanwhile Aitaraj and Rambahadur crept closer and closer to the building. It was to be their task to see whether there were any Germans there or not. They seemed to be away hours but time moved so slowly that I was surprised to find on looking at my watch that they were away for less than half an hour.

" No one there, Sahib. We threw a stone in through the window of the bottom room and although I didn't go inside we waited for about ten minutes. I am sure that the house is completely empty".

I spoke to Lance Naik Bilbahadur Tamang, the commander of the escort section. There was no need to give him lengthy instructions when these had been discussed earlier that day. His men were to stay in their present positions until I flashed a tiny torchlight out of the top window, the one that faced the Battalion lines. Then they were to return to the Battalion until the following evening.

It was not as quiet an evening as the one when we had made our previous visit to the farmhouse. Here and there, especially from the neighbouring battalion's sector, there was desultory firing with a few crump crumps of mortars which sounded as if they were German. Nothing stirred in our immediate area. Aitaraj lead the way to the house. The door was on the other side, the German side. As we neared it Aitaraj repeated his stone throwing act and once again the three of us waited for a minute or two. All clear. We moved towards the house. On reaching the door I grabbed Aitaraj's arm and whispered to him to wait a second while I shone the torch to see if there were any booby traps or mines. Although the torch was a tiny one, I took the precaution of shading the beam, moved it up and down and then inside the door. We found nothing. Inside there was a table with a few old tins and a very stale piece of bread on it. The atmosphere of the room smelt nasty and dirty, stuffy from a complete lack of ventilation. No one had opened windows after the Italian farmer had left his home in haste when the foreigners began to fight for possesion of his farm. The shutters of the windows of the bottom room, except for the one through which Aitaraj had thrown his stone, were tightly closed which accentuated the smell of things unwashed and unclean. Protected by a sentry outside, assisted by another observer in the room upstairs, the German patrols had obviously considered it safe to eat and smoke in this room : the collection of debris and numerous stub ends of cigarettes showed that they had paid several visits to the farmhouse. It was a sad place, quite unworthy of its courtesy title, Windsor Castle.

Rambahadur followed me up the steep wooden steps which led to a large room, with a smaller room leading off to the left. Previous occupants had knocked out the window frames to improve observation in three directions : the large room was the one the Germans had been using to gaze at the Indians and Gurkhas on the other side of the valley. Rambahadur went to call Aitaraj while I, using a compass, began to orientate myself with known landmarks. As the moon had waned considerably since our last visit, I was not able to come to any startling conclusions except the obvious one, that the morning light would reveal much of interest.

Aitaraj set up his wireless and after fiddling with the knobs was keen to talk to Battalion headquarters. Permission was not granted. He was told to listen in on the Battalion ' net'. After turning the volume down, he reported that the reception of other radio stations was remarkably clear. Outside the house everything remained quiet. I was not keen to send Lance Naik Bilbahadur and his men away but realised that they must be allowed sufficient time for their return journey. If they moved at speed, without taking the normal precautions they might walk into an ambush. It was nearly three o'clock. I decided to make them wait another quarter of an hour before flashing the signal to tell them to begin moving. The time passed and the world around us continued to be peaceful. I gave the signal to Bilbahadur.

In my experience men are at their lowest ebb during the last hour of darkness when black night slowly turns to the cold grey light of dawn. So it was in the farmhouse. The temperature dropped and the three of us felt deflated as the tension and excitement of the past few hours drained away. The thought of spending nearly fifteen hours in the house depressed me ; I sensed without asking the two Gurkhas, that they envied Bilbahadur and his men who would be back with their friends already. It was at such a moment that we heard noises and voices—and the owners of the voices were approaching the house from the rear, the German side. The Gurkhas looked at me. " Dushman", whispered Rambahadur, " What shall we do, Sahib ?"

I motioned him to keep quiet. We listened, and heard someone enter the room below, banging things on the table. Outside the window two Germans began to speak in undertones : One appeared to be giving instructions because the other voice kept on repeating monotonously ' Ja, ja'.

I can remember thinking, ' so this is the end of my war. I am to be a prisoner. Or should we attack them first and try and make a bolt for it'? I searched for a solution but in truth I was crushed by fear, my mind was wracked with indecision. Aitaraj crawled near to breathe a whisper in my ear : " Don't you think we should throw grenades at them first, Sahib ? They are bound to come up here in a few minutes' time".

" We don't know that, nor do we know how many there are or where the others may be. They might be a patrol just calling in here before moving on".

Then there was a buzzing noise from Aitaraj's radio.

" For God's sake switch that damned set off".

Aitaraj did so. In the meantime I had motioned Rambahadur to sit at the top of the steps at one side, with a grenade in his hand, pin out ready to drop it down into the room below, should anyone begin to climb up towards our hiding place. Tensely we sat, trying not to move, fighting back coughs. Dawn was now breaking. Still we could hear the man below. He lit a fire because smoke wafted up ; probably brewing some tea. The men outside had either moved away or were sitting in silence waiting for their morning brew up. I took Rambahadur's place, gripping the lever of the grenade in my hand when he passed it to me. Aitaraj had taken up a position by the window on the German side, ready to open fire or hurl a hand grenade or both if necessary. Behind him Rambahadur looked tense and frightened then, with a shy smile of apology at me, he opened his flies and urinated where he sat. I felt a similar urge to follow his example but fought it off while acting as guard above the steps.

Any thought of carrying out the mission given us by the Brigadier was forgotten. The sun rose and with it the smell of dry and drying human excretia became more and more powerful. In the past our enemies had found it necessary to relieve themselves near their post of duty. Then, as Rambahadur was taking over from me again, we heard the door below shut. A few shuffling noises outside, then there was silence.

Aitaraj beckoned me to come near him.

'' Dushman is going, Sahib''; there he was, a man in a grey uniform walking down a path towards some bushes. He disappeared. Everything was still.

'' We are safe, Sahib'' whispered Ramahadur, more in hope than with conviction. I warned them that we would be wise to wait about half an hour before doing anything that might make too much noise. I agreed to Aitaraj opening his set again while Rambahadur and I each took a window to maintain a watch. By now it was a beautiful day and apart from intermittent shelling near the coast, the whole front was quiet. On such a morning as this many of the officers and men off duty would be sitting in the sun, enjoying the warmth while others would be airing blankets or drying washing near outposts and hideouts. I began to feel hungry and indicated by signals to my companions that they could begin eating the biscuits and chocolate we had brought with us. A mug of hot tea would have been much more welcome but we had to be content with tepid water from the bottles carried on our belts. We ate the cold snack in silence, trying to forget the unpleasant smells around us. Through the left hand window I could see B Company's position with remarkable clarity and by using binoculars, noticed some Gurkha soldiers moving around. No wonder they had suffered several casualties from mortars recently. I marked on my map the points which could be seen so clearly from the house. I was able to warn the company commander next day and this saved further casualties.

I asked Rambahadur if he had seen anything yet out of the other window. He was using another pair of binoculars to search the clump of trees behind which the German had disappeared.

'' I have seen the occasional movement over there, a bit of grey, now and then a wisp of smoke. Do you think they have got a position there, Sahib ?''

I beckoned Rambahadur to change places. For several minutes I searched the area with his glasses. Tired eyes and tense nerves told me that there were some figures moving behind the trees but I could not be one hundred per cent certain. I did not want to ask the British guns to open fire at the area until our supicions were confirmed. Nevertheless, I thought it would be wise to give the gunners a warning so I wrote a short message, ending with a statement that the executive order to fire might follow at any moment. After reading the message, Aitaraj began to spell it out in morse which was considerably quieter than relaying it by voice over the radio. So quickly did his fingers tap out the message that I assumed that someone at the other end was receiving him. I was wrong. After a few minutes, Aitaraj took his earphones off to report in exasperation :

" I can hear them ; Battalion are talking to A Company but no one seems to hear me".

" Keep on trying. They are probably concentrating on each other's transmissions and haven't picked you up. There may be a real break in a minute, then you'll get through".

The Lance Naik nodded, albeit without any confidence and tried once more. Soon it was evident from his expression that he was having no success. Once more he took off his headset to carry out a careful check of his radio set. It was no good : it was not transmitting. Much of the patrol's value was lost already. From his forlorn expression I realised that Aitaraj was blaming himself, no doubt feeling that he had let us down.

I knelt beside him and put a hand on his shoulder : " Don't worry, Aite, it's not your fault. You may have knocked something on the way out, anyway these sets are always temperamental".

All we could do was to make the best out of a bad job. I decided that we would open a log book in which all incidents would be recorded ; timings, approximate map references and our assessments of things seen and heard. I had just finished explaining what we were to do when, seemingly outside the house, a heavy mortar began firing. We could see puffs of smoke rising from the location we had been scrutinising with such care for over an hour. Obviously the men we had seen and heard were a mortar crew who, having fired their salvo of bombs, might well move again so as to escape retaliation from the British.

" Dear God, why did that set have to go ' dis' now ? We would have been able to give a pin-point reference on those chaps and they would have got it in the neck—I bet Battalion are swearing blue murder at us—listen in again, Aite".

He did so. They were. We could hear Alan's voice using veiled speech, imploring call sign ' Charlie O1' to answer and acknowledge his signals. His voice became more and more irritated but there was nothing we could do. It was a bitter moment in a frustrating position ; if one of my Gurkhas had begun crying I believe I would have added my tears of wrath. However there was no point in lamenting further : using a compass I took an accurate fix on the German mortar position and scribbled notes in the improvised logbook.

The German mortar stopped firing, Rambahadur asked if I thought that they would move towards the house and if so what were we to do. I agreed that if they did then we would be in danger once more. However, I hoped that if our guns opened up in retaliation then the enemy mortar team would not risk coming to such a conspicuous landmark as our house.

'' Let's hope you are right, Sahib'' was Rambahadur's reply.

I was right. We heard the distant ' pop pop' of our own Battalion mortars then a few seconds later the crump crump of the bombs as they landed a few hundred yards away to the left. Unfortunately although the direction was correct, the bombs fell well short of the enemy hiding place. We, the observers, could do nothing to correct the error. It seemed certain that the counter bombardment would move the Germans on but which way would they go ? Would they come towards the house to use it for observation during the rest of the day ? Or would they think it too obvious a target ?

Time passed slowly ; each minute passed gave us a little more confidence. Perhaps after all the Germans had sought shelter elsewhere.

After the patrol was over, I recorded the highlights and dramatic moments so that years later it has not been difficult to reconstruct the outline of the story. The notes served to stimulate my recollections of the day and night spent in Windsor Castle. The period after the mortar stopped firing was covered by two sentences hence my memory about the afternoon period is hazy.

After midday we relaxed a little in the belief that the worst was over. We had begun to put our faith in the fact that the farmhouse was continually under surveillance from two observation points on the Battalion front and hence suspected the Germans would not risk being shelled during daylight. They had never done so in the past : it was unlikely that they would do so that day.

As there was no point in the three of us gazing out of the two rear windows, I decided that each man in turn could rest for an hour. It was not easy for the observers to keep awake because the afternoon was hot and not having slept at all during the night, meant eyes heavy with fatigue. Rambahadur nodded off. I shook his arm roughly then five minutes later felt Rambahadur doing the same to me, not quite so roughly but with a satisfied grin on his face.

Behind us with his head on a brick, Aitaraj was fast asleep, his snores breaking the silence. ' Lucky beggar', I can remember thinking because I was not one who could turn sleep on and off when excited or frightened by events around me. At the end of the hour, Rambahadur shook the Lance Naik into some kind of wakefulness and was not slow in using the same hard pillow for his hour's rest. Aitaraj and I kept up an intermittent conversation trying to keep each other awake. As the afternoon wore on dozens of huge black flies appeared and these buzzed and attacked us : they even roused Rambahadur who swotted at them ineffectually with his hands in anger. In the end he gave it up and borrowed my binoculars to look back at the comparatively safe haven of rest on the other side of the river, occupied by men of the Battalion.

Before the sun began to set, one or two Germans were seen at a distance going about their business : they appeared to be getting ready to move forward into listening posts and static patrols near the British lines or preparing for other nocturnal activities. The Gurkhas passed on their observations to me : I recorded everything seen including an estimate of location and their assessment of the significance of each spotting. We were busy until the dark shadows of evening made the task impossible. By now I realised that the Brigadier's assessment of the importance of Windsor Castle, to both sides, was an accurate one. Later, next day, I was foolish enough to give such an opinion in the Brigadier's presence and, as a consequence we had to make a third and final visit to the insalubrious farmhouse.

Lance Naik Bilbahadur had been told to bring his men back to the same position they had occupied the night before. As they could not begin moving from the Battalion before dark, then it was unlikely that they would reach Windsor Castle before 9 o'clock. This aspect of the operation had not been well considered. My Gurkha companions and I now realised that it was much more likely that the Germans would arrive in or near the house before Bilbahadur did. I can remember thinking what a bloody fool I had been. I realised that Bilbahadur should have been told to stay at the river to protect us when we reached the fording place. He could have reached there quite quickly. I voiced these thoughts to the others who were as jittery as I was.

'' We can't stay here, Sahib, until Bilbahadur comes, it would be madness''.

This was Airataraj, Rambahadur nodded his assent. I replied : '' Okay. I feel the same but remember we might be shot by Bilbahadur or his men because they will not be expecting to meet anyone who is friendly on their way over here''.

It was a valid point, one that could not be disregarded. When men are on patrol in the dark they are tense and inclined to shoot on suspicion because he who fires first usually survives. In reply to a suggestion from Aitaraj ' We could make a little more noise than usual', I pointed out that there could well be German patrols within yards of us. Tense, nervy and frightened we sought a solution to our predicament.

I have often wondered what we would have done if the darkness around us had remained quiet and undisturbed. It did not, however. Suddenly Rambahadur spotted four figures who were silhouetted against the skyline about three hundred yards from the rear of the house. He pointed them out, saying '' They are coming this way— let's go, Sahib''.

In retrospect, I cannot remember even giving permission and certainly I gave no orders because I had the same uncontrollable urge to get out of the house and run like the wind towards the Battalion lines.

We were down the steps, out of the back door and away, forgetting
the well proven rule and oft-practised discipline which patrols were
urged to adopt if they were going to escape attention of enemy listeners. We ran expecting someone to open fire on us from behind but
fortune favoured the three reckless and less than brave men. Only the
river halted our hurried retreat, to bring me back to my senses. I
began to restrain the others when, out of the darkness, came an
angry Bilbahadur.

" What the hell are you doing, Sahib ? We so very nearly shot you
all. We saw what we thought to be a ' dushman' patrol coming down
the hill and I put my men in an ambush position. Luckily I told them
that I would fire the first shot and was just going to do so when I
heard your voice".

The above in an expurgated version of what the angry Gurkha
said. It was full of Nepali expletives which would lose much of their
venom if translated into English. I had no experience of being lashed
in anger by a Gurkha's tongue. My indifferent understanding of the
Nepali language meant that I missed much of what was being said
although I guessed the meaning. Fortunately Aitaraj took Bilbahadur
to one side and cooled him down : much of his anger had been
shock after realising how close to a tragedy we had been ; sheer
relief had caused him to give vent to feelings of rage.

The whole party turned to move slowly in a controlled manner
towards B Company's outpost with Lance Naik Bilbahadur taking
charge. When we heard the quiet challenge of the sentry, I felt like
shouting aloud in joy. Our ordeal was over. The Gurkhas went back
to their billet while I made my way to Battalion Headquarters. From
there I phoned back a short interim report to Brigade. I was told that
the Brigadier was away but would see me next day, after I had had a
good rest. Meanwhile our Commanding Officer had gone forward to
visit a company where Alan contacted him to pass on the news of the
patrol's safe return. He put the phone down : " Desmond says you
are to have a strong drink on him. Let's get away from these wire-
lesses and go into the rest room". Next door we met the medical
officer, a fine man, much admired by all ranks for his gentleness and
deep compassion towards his patients as well as for his courage and
unselfish behaviour under fire. Doctor Gerald Sausman was an
Anglo-Indian who unlike many of his kind never pretended to be
anything else and was accepted without any reservations by British
officers and Gurkha soldiers alike. All respected and admired him and
in the heat of battle had cause to love him.

The only other man in the rest room was a red-faced, middle aged
major, who was a stranger to me. He was introduced by Alan as
Major Gordon from the 10th Gurkhas. We shook hands while
Gerald Sausman produced a bottle of whisky and some glasses. The

warmth, the whisky, and the relaxed companionship of the three men helped to unwind nerves that had been overstretched, courage that had been overtaxed. I felt glad to be alive and gradually the nightmare of Windsor Castle was forgotten as the others joked and made light of the experiences I related to them. Under normal circumstances two whiskies were not a big or unusual dose of alcohol for me. But I had not slept for forty-eight hours : many stresses and strains had been experienced during that time. Fortunately I realised that another drink would be lethal—although Alan pressed me hard. Gerald supported my refusal. Moreover, Major Gordon had begun to irritate me by asking rather naive questions about the way I conducted our patrol operations. I felt that the older man was quoting the text book at me without having any battle experience behind him. Losing patience I asked Gordon if he had ever taken a ' real' patrol out and saw that my question had annoyed him. The Major muttered an angry reply and went away. Alan's eyebrows went up, he whispered, '' You've put up a black, old boy''.

I felt it was time to go to bed. Gerald Sausman accompanied me to my room which was just as well as outside in the cold air everything seemed to go black, and the Doctor's arm was needed to half support and half carry me to my bed. '' Don't get up till you've had a good rest, Birdie ; no, you are not drunk—you have just run out of steam, only sleep can put you right. Here is a sleeping pill but don't take it until you really have to''. I thanked him and apologised for being rude to a stranger—who was he, anyway ? Gerald smiled. '' Don't worry about it now, you'll find that he's a good chap really. He had better be because he's going to take over from Desmond as our Commanding Officer''.

'' Dear God, and I was rude to the old so and so—hope he doesn't post me away without consulting Desmond first. Oh well, Doc, he's seen me at my worst. I'm far more worried about what that damned Brigadier is going to say tomorrow. Good night''.

Next day it was officially announced that Major Gerry Gordon was to take over from Desmond forthwith. It was not totally unexpected as the latter had been appointed in an emergency during the Cassino battles and under the circumstances could hardly have expected to retain command. There were many others senior to him awaiting promotion to Lieutenant Colonel. Being a cheerful Irishman Desmond took it all philosophically, his only stipulation being that he wanted to go to a rifle company rather than sit ' on my arse' as Battalion second-in-command in B Echelon'. His request was granted.

Gerry Gordon's greeting to me at breakfast was cordial. No mention was made by either of us about the previous night's conversation. Major Gerry Gordon, soon to be a Lieutenant Colonel, was a highly strung man with an inferiority complex which quickly became apparent. It was not his fault that he had yet to see active service, he was acutely aware that the officers of his new Battalion, all much younger than he was and none of them ' Regulars', had been through the mill at Cassino. He was especially keen on training and as days passed his true qualities were to be appreciated by all ranks in the Battalion. His nervous volatile temperament did not conceal for long a warm hearted affection for the Gurkha soldiers he had served with for several years. A gentle humane man, our new Commanding Officer had all the qualities of an excellent commander except one : he cared too much for his Gurkhas so that casualties caused him to grieve and indulge in bouts of self recrimination, and he often found himself guilty. Such a weakness was to prove his undoing as a commander but it never cost him the respect and affection of those who served under his command.

Before I went to Brigade Headquarters Desmond had a word with me in the presence of Gerry Gordon. Desmond had had several tussles with Brigadier Hawke who was earning himself a reputation as a ' push on regardless' type of commander. Without saying so in as many words or displaying blatant disloyalty about his superior to a junior officer, Desmond advised me to speak my mind and not allow myself to be pushed into any rash foolhardy enterprise.

Although a wise warning it was not so easy for a twenty-year-old subaltern to stand his ground when confronted by an over-enthusiastic Brigadier as I was to discover that morning. At first I basked in the older man's rather fulsome praise. Brigadier Hawke went on : Yes, the patrol report was excellent, just what he had expected ; Windsor Castle had been used with impunity for too long by the Gerry who had thus inflicted unnecessary casualties on us as a result ; from my report the Germans obviously had a small base probably four or five hundred yards away from the farmhouse : while it would be unwise to send another reconnaissance patrol out, surely it was an excellent opportunity to take some offensive action against the unsuspecting Germans ? He spoke with enthusiastic fervour, but was, he maintained, only thinking aloud—and what were Smith's views ?

Bewildered by such a flow of rhetoric I found it difficult to think of anything to say that sounded convincing. Not knowing what the Brigadier had in mind by ' some offensive action' I found little encouragement to be very forthcoming.

Remembering Desmond's warning, I gave my opinion that the Germans must have seen us make our hurried exit from the house although they had not fired at the three fleeing figures. It might be wise to wait a few days before revisiting ' Windsor Castle'—for whatever purpose the Brigadier had in mind.

Brigadier Hawke accepted this with reluctance although he made it quite clear that he was not going to shelve his proposals for long. He let me go with a promise that ' something would be cooked up' he would speak to my new Commanding Officer on the following day.

Realising that my stalwarts, Aitaraj and Rambahadur, might have to make yet another visit to the same area, I excluded them from all patrol activities during the next four nights. They had earned a break which the two Gurkhas enjoyed to the full. So, indeed, should I have done but I was still wound up, a bundle of nerves, sleeping badly. Every time one of my patrols went out, I found sleep impossible until the men returned. Gerald Sausman gave me a stern warning : '' If you don't relax, Birdie, you will have a breakdown. I will talk to the CO if you continue like this. You look like the ghost of Banquo''. I begged him not to say anything, to wait until the next big show had been completed. With obvious misgivings the Doctor agreed, stipulating that he would wait no more than a week. If I was in the same state then, nothing would stop him approaching Colonel Gordon.

In the meantime the Colonel, having heard my report about the latest visit to Brigade Headquarters, had decided to see the Brigadier himself. Without wishing in any way to fall out with his superior at their first meeting, Gerry Gordon tried to make it clear that he was against his Battalion patrols being briefed and debriefed by officers in Brigade HQ. It was against normal military practice. That point was conceded, reluctantly, by Brigadier Hawke who promised to give him an outline plan and then let Gordon himself alter or amend it as he saw fit.

The two men parted, neither confident that they would work well in harmony. Hawke had the feeling that Gordon would be unduly worried by casualties and setbacks : the Commanding Officer had the suspicion that his Brigadier was too ambitious, determined to get on whatever the cost. During the following three months events were to prove that there was much truth in both these opinions.

Three days passed before Alan Howard warned me that the Colonel would be briefing me later that morning. The patrol would go out during the following night and all members of the platoon would be involved.

This is the story of how a subaltern at times withstood, and at others failed to resist, the pressures imposed on him by war. If a graph had been drawn to show the state of my morale throughout 1944, the period covering late April and early May would have displayed a violent pendulum of ups and downs. My moods alternated between an unnatural sense of dare-devilry and moments of deep doubt and depression. There were times when I felt that I was a sham, a phoney who was acting the part of a dashing young officer. When the darker clouds of despair passed, I became talkative, cracking jokes and being far more noisy than usual. Gerald Sausman was not fooled by my newly acquired effervescence but was reluctant to break his promise about keeping silence. Nevertheless, the doctor felt he had a duty to the Battalion which transcended our friendship so he decided to tackle the problem in a different way. Unbeknown to me, he sought out the Colonel and suggested that if the Patrol platoon was to continue in being for some time to come, then it might be wise to think of a relief for Birdie Smith—and as the impending operation might be a hazardous one would it not be a good idea if his designated relief went with him to see how things were done ?

Colonel Gerry Gordon took the point although he made it clear that he now had reservations about keeping the Patrol ' gladiators' in being for much longer. He disliked the concept, recognising that in theory there were advantages but feeling that in practice it put far too much strain on a few individuals. Later I was to agree with the Colonel's assessment. I came to admit that I had been living in a dream, at the mercy of a mental whirlpool which was spinning me round and around.

Although the climax of the third patrol is imprinted with an astonishing clarity on my mind to this day, I cannot remember any details of the briefing I received—in complete contrast to the patrols which have already been described. I cannot explain why there are such gaps in my memory. Confirmed facts are scanty therefore. The patrol platoon was to use ' Windsor Castle' as a temporary base to launch a raid against the enemy mortar positions, noted by us during the second patrol. Another group of men, commanded by Lieutenant ' Gunnar' Keightly, was to come out later but I cannot remember for what reason or at what stage in the operation. The temptation to guess and produce fictitious reasons has been resisted.

The members of the platoon were not over-enthusiastic about the operation, probably because they realised the Germans had good reason to be on their guard and suspicious about the 'Windsor Castle' area. Although my Gurkhas were delighted to hear that they would be allowed to do some fighting, by choice they would have preferred to have been given another assignment. I finished inspecting my team and found them alert and ready for anything, but sensed that they shared my feelings of misgiving. In later years I was to write that : ' We were all apprehensive about the operation without knowing why. The portents seemed favourable but none of us was raring to go '.

At first all went as planned or to be more accurate, I cannot recollect any important incident happening until we had reached ' Windsor Castle'; on finding it empty we set up a temporary headquarters within the house. This time the radio functioned efficiently so that communications were established with Battalion Headquarters. Three protection patrols were sent out in different directions, all of which reported that no Germans had been seen or heard.

Behind us the Battalion sector, too, was quiet. Earlier that day a theory had been expounded by higher headquarters that the enemy was preparing to withdraw along the whole Adriatic sector, to conform with events on the other side of Italy. Certainly for the first hour or two of the patrol nothing occurred to refute such an appreciation by the ' top brass.'

In the downstairs room, with the windows closed so that torch lights could be used to look at maps and to use the wireless, my designated successor, Matt Molloy and I began to plan the next stage of the operation. A strong raiding party was to search for and, if found, destroy the German mortars in the site nearby. If the enemy were there in numbers then fire support from Allied guns and mortars would be brought down by a quick request over the radio.

Molloy was three years older than I was and quite the opposite to me in temperament. He loved to be the centre of everything, a cheerful extrovert who enjoyed life to the full. Being an excellent mimic he was the life and soul of any party with a fund of stories suitable for a male audience. Although I liked Matt when we were on our own, I kept my distance when other officers were present. In my mind there was a suspicion that the gay joker was not such a dashing fellow as he pretended to be but I never voiced such thoughts to anyone except Gerald, the Doctor. During this night our early relationship had been excellent which surprised me a little because I was younger and junior to Molloy. However, on the Colonel's express instructions I had been told to command the operation with Molloy being present as an observer. In retrospect, it was not surprising that this untidy arrangement proved to be a strain for both of us.

If events up to midnight have been dimmed by the passing years the two explosions from seemingly outside the back door have not been forgotten, the first a deep note followed by another sharp crack that went off a few seconds later. Then silence. It was unnecessary to tell the men inside the building to put out the lights ; it had been done automatically while we stood, listened and waited. Matt and I looked at each other. '' Mines'' whispered Matt, '' What the hell ?. I'll take a look from upstairs''. Matt climbed up the steps leading to the top room to ask the sentry there if he had seen anything. Meanwhile, I went outside to question the men who had been guarding the house when the explosions occurred. They gave varying estimates of the distance, with some saying two hundred and others up to four hundred yards away. All were convinced that the noises had been caused by two types of mines.

For a few minutes it remained a mystery. If there were any Germans nearby, then undoubtedly they would have been alerted and would probably send someone to investigate. Certainly there did not seem to be much chance of the next phase of the operation being carried out against an enemy ready for any emergency.

Back inside the room Matt and I compared our findings. Matt reported that the sentry upstairs had seen the flashes which appeared to come from the path used by the whole patrol about an hour earlier that evening. Like the men outside, the sentry was convinced that two mines had been detonated. But by whom ? There were no stray cattle in No-man's-land ; the Seventh Gurkhas had not placed mines in front of their Company positions ; and if the Germans had done so, surely they would have kept clear of that path thereafter ? And, as Matt said, if there had been mines on the path earlier how the hell had twenty-five people walked through them unscathed ?

We decided to let the Colonel know because the sound of the explosions would have been heard on the other side of the valley. He would have to be warned that any chance of surprise had been lost already.

'' The Germans will be buzzing round here like angry hornets'', was Matt's gloomy prediction. I asked him to speak to the Colonel on the radio while I organised a reception for the Germans who might be visiting the house at any moment. While looking for Lance Naik Bilbahadur, I heard voices raised above the normal undertones used at night when unfriendly ears are known to be within shooting distance. They were speaking in Gurkhali and were obviously excited. In anger I strode towards the group of men, telling them to shut up unless they wished to be clobbered by the Germans.

'' Keightly Sahib has been wounded by a mine. I was ahead of him when the second mine went off. The rest of the men are back with him, not daring to move any further forward along the path ''. The speaker was Ramsing. I asked him how he escaped. He replied : '' Because I knew the way, Sahib told me to be the leading scout. After the second mine went off the Sahib shouted to me not to come back but to tell, you what had happened. The other men will have to carry him back to B Company''. I asked him if Keightly was badly wounded. '' I don't know, I was well ahead of him. Jangbir said that the Sahib's leg was smashed but he was still giving out orders when I left''.

My thoughts came in a rush, in no logical sequence. First, anger because 'Gunnar' Keightly had come far too early and anyway should not have been using the same route as we had done. That had been agreed during the final briefing in the lines. Then deep shock because of my friend's plight, followed by fear that we would all be attacked at any moment.

I went to consult Matt who took off the earphones to ask what had happened. In the flickering light of a small stubby candle, I could see that Matt was as shaken by the news as I had been.

'' There were no mines on that path when we came up. The

bastards must have put them down after we arrived here'', was his opinion. I agreed. I also felt that it would be wise if we got out of the house quickly and sat tight for a short while. It was pointless for us to charge round until we saw what Gerry was going to do. '' God alone knows whether it will be possible to do anything after that''.

'' Agreed—what about Gunnar ? Hadn't one of us better go and check that the ' bods' are evacuating him back to the lines quickly ?'' asked Matt.

I had been ducking this issue, dreading that he would ask the question. I had been fighting shy of something which had been in my mind as soon as Ramsing had reported the gloomy news. I told Aitaraj to summon Ramsing. Looking at Matt I remember saying : '' Who is to go ? You, I believe, because I'm in charge and we could be attacked here at any time''.

The older officer did not reply. We continued to look at each other. I thought, ' You're afraid, afraid of mines and, dear God, so am I. You know that I am shit scared, too—we're both bloody cowards'.

Ramsing came in. I asked him if he thought the other members of the escort would get Keightly Sahib back quickly. Yes, was his reply. There were five of them under the command of Lance Naik Jangbir. No, he didn't think it was necessary for anyone to go down the track.

The Rifleman's reply afforded the let out his two officers were seeking, although I was uneasy about accepting, without demur, advice given by a young Gurkha Rifleman. Ramsing had been badly frightened ; moreover, he was feeling guilty because he had led the escort party up the wrong path in direct contravention of the original orders he had been given when selected to act as their guide.

Molloy told Battalion Headquarters that the wounded Keightly was being carried back by the escort patrol and added that we were moving out of the house in case the Germans attacked—he obtained permission to close down the radio until it was safe to re-establish communications. Meanwhile I had begun to move the patrol away, to the east of the house where we could continue observing ' Windsor Castle' and, if necessary, defend ourselves against German patrols.

The men on patrol did not require any orders to remain alert or maintain absolute silence. All were keyed up to expect the worst, praying that they would not be kept in suspense for too long. During the first half hour there were several false alarms as ' Dushman' sightings were reported ; one or two may have been genuine, but the others were the figments of excited imaginations.

Matt Molloy, always an impatient, restless man, began to fidget. He suggested that we should carry on with the original mission or, alternatively, get to hell out of it back to the Battalion lines. Such thoughts had been in my mind too. While it required courage to go forward it was almost impossible to pull back because, apart from the two explosions, the Germans had not interfered with us in any way. How could we justify a withdrawal when there was no evidence to show that we were in danger ?

It had to be forward then. The decision was relayed back to Battalion headquarters by radio, Aitaraj passing the message in morse so as to avoid a noisy transmission by voice. A laconic ' Roger' in reply gave us no indication of the Colonel's feelings except that, rightly, he was leaving the final decision to us. There was no time for discussion anyway as the night was passing. Given time and normal circumstances, I would have preferred to send a small reconnaissance patrol into the danger area before moving forward with some twenty odd men. Lack of time precluded such tactics ; we would have to chance our luck, accepting that more noise was inevitable. Although I was nominally in command, the relationship with my designated successor senior in rank as well as in years, was beginning to be an unhappy one. Matt accused me of being over cautious while I retorted that Molloy would dash into anything without using his brains first. In spite of our disagreement I insisted on retaining overall command of the patrol, much to Molloy's annoyance.

I split the patrol into two parties, each of twelve men. Matt volunteered to take his ahead with my group moving slightly to the rear on the right flank. We would move on a compass bearing for about a six hundred yards which, according to our estimates, would bring us near to the clump of trees which the Germans had used during my second visit to ' Windsor Castle'.

More than that we could not plan. 'A reconnaissance in force' was Matt's opinion. I thought it was a wild leap in the dark—I did not like it one little bit. Events, however, were to support Matt's assessment because unbeknown to us the Germans had moved away after the mines exploded, deciding it would be easier to bring down a mortar strike against any snoopers rather than using men to ambush them with grenades and small arms fire.

Which they did—with Teutonic efficiency. Our patrol had gone about three hundred yards when two verey lights went up to our front. We froze in our tracks. As the lights flashed and spluttered in the sky above, I swore because I could see our two groups were clearly visible in the bright naked light. I sensed that we could be for it now ; aloud I told the men around me to drop flat as soon as the lights dimmed before going out. Matt and his men were a few yards ahead so it was impossible to communicate with them—all I could hope was that Matt would make a similar assessment. As the artificial light above us flickered and then died, we threw ourselves to the ground, wondering if the Germans had seen us, and if so, what would follow. We were not kept waiting long ; the Germans were adept at bringing down accurate mortar fire in a matter of seconds, and this they did. Crump crump crump—down came the bombs squealing and whining with hate before exploding into splinters of jagged metal which ricochetted round the defenceless members of my patrol. It took me a second or two to realise that though we were far too near for comfort, it was Matt's group that had been spotted by the Germans ; bombs seemed to be landing where they had gone to ground. The 'stonk' went on for about five minutes, the noise was deafening ; there was nothing to do except hope, pray and hug the earth.

The hymn of hate turned off like a tap of water. One minute there was sound and fury, the next silence. There was no time to lose if we were going to avoid another dose of punishment. No one had been hurt in my party so I ordered them to go back about a hundred yards where we waited for Matt. A minute or two later, two or three Gurkhas appeared out of the darkness. I asked them what had happened and where was the Sahib. '' The Sahib's all right. Two of the lads have been badly wounded. Molloy Sahib would like you to cover us while we carry them back''. They went back to help and I told my men to take up fire positions. A few minutes later Molloy appeared. '' Give me five minutes and then beatle back to another covering position. I think 62 Balbahadur Rai has ' had it'. His head is not a pretty sight but we can't leave him here, dead or alive''.

'' Do you need any of my men to help with the carrying ?''.

'' No, we have enough. I'd much rather have you guarding our backs. I'm going to make for A Company rather than use the ' Windsor Castle' path. Can Aitaraj get on to them ?''

'' Yes, but not here. He'd better move with you and use his radio when you take a breather—before going down to the river, I suggest''. Off they went.

One of the wounded was making loud wailing noises, groaning in terrible pain. There were no stretchers. Obviously Matt would have given both morphia injections but the men faced a harrowing ordeal, however careful the carriers were. 62 Balbahadur Rai did not survive the journey and the A Company sentry who challenged Matt's men saw the lifeless body of his friend carried in. Balbahadur had been in his section before volunteering to join the Patrol platoon.

The Germans allowed us to withdraw to safety without taking any steps to stop or harass us. At the time such welcome forbearance was difficult to understand. Later it became evident that they were about to begin a complete withdrawal across the Adriatic sector. For this reason, our patrol had been stopped before we could find out the whole story.

The patrol's return to A Company, something that took about two hours, can be summarised in one phrase ; it passed without any more incidents. I spoke to Alan on the field telephone from A Company to give the Intelligence officer an outline report about our adventures. Then I asked if I could speak to Gerald Sausman. The Doctor sounded grave. Keightly's left leg had been amputated and his general condition was serious. Far more serious than it ought to have been, he added. After I asked him to explain, Gerald replied with words that I have never forgotten. '' The poor devil lost a lot of blood—whatever were you doing—a small field dressing put on badly, no attempt at a tourniquet. Just think of the hours I've spent trying to teach everyone in the Battalion the simple rudiments of first aid. If he dies, well. . . ''. Stabs of guilt caused me to ask again if he was really as seriously wounded as all that.

'' Even the body of a tough, fit young man can only take a certain amount of punishment. It is going to be touch and go, I fear. Anyway, would you like to come to the MRS with me to see him ? I'm going directly after morning sick parade''.

All thoughts about the patrol were completely overshadowed by the news about ' Gunnar'. After agreeing to go with Gerald, I told Matt the gloomy news. A shocked Matt murmured, '' Gunnar' losing a leg, poor sod. I'm sure he'll pull through. he's a tough customer''.

'' Let's hope so. More than anyone else, you and I should be praying overtime''. Matt flushed in anger. He did not like the remark one little bit. For a moment I thought he was going to hit me, then turning away, Molloy said : '' Look chum. You were in charge, which you kept telling me ad nauseam while we were out there. I'm not saying anything to anyone, but don't ram your conscience down my throat again—ever''. Thereafter the relationship between us remained coldly polite and distant : we never spoke about the patrol to each other or to anyone else in the Battalion.

At Battalion headquarters, the Colonel listened to my report in silence. Now I realise that he was worried by my over-wrought manner, sympathetically aware that the casualties had sapped my self confidence. After I finished, Gerry Gordon remarked that the patrol could not have escaped without suffering casualties, whatever decisions I had taken.

I told Colonel Gerry that I was going with the Doctor to see ' Gunnar' Keightly.

'' Fine, and then you and your men will be given a real rest.'' I thanked him, then said I would like to be relieved at once ; not only because of the recent patrol, but because I was not sleeping properly ; '' Doc Sausman has been getting at me for some time now''.

The Colonel smiled, '' I know, he told me. Don't worry, because I have decided to disband the Patrol platoon, anyway. Any day now we will be advancing so that there is no further use for the platoon. Off you go. Gerald is waiting for you''.

Normally I would have been annoyed with Gerald for having spoken to the CO before the appointed time. Now I felt grateful to him for his intervention because it made an interview that could have been embarrassing remarkably easy. I thanked Gerald who smiled, said nothing, and then began driving the jeep furiously towards the MRS in Lanciano.

At the MRS, Gerald went to find the surgeon, saying that he would join me later in ' Gunnar's' ward. I felt like crying out : '' Don't leave me. I cannot face Gunnar alone. I feel so full of guilt and remorse''. I sensed that the Doctor knew about the turmoil in my mind but was determined to make me meet Gunnar on my own.

The QA Sister, in charge of the officers' ward, gave me permission to visit my friend, adding that Keightly might be asleep and, if he was, then on no account was the patient to be woken. Having said this she then accompanied me to ensure compliance with her instructions.

Gunnar's eyes were closed. Above his head there was a large bottle of blood. He was still having a transfusion. The QA put a finger to her lips. I nodded. The wounded man was behind a mosquito net, presumably to keep flies away as the MRS was accommodated in a building never intended to house a hospital. Keightly was breathing heavily but looked peaceful—perhaps too peaceful, I felt, as we stood in silence beside his bed. I found myself praying ' Dear God let me be forgiven. Let Gunnar live. I have failed him once. Give me a chance to make amends.'

There was a soft touch on my arm. I looked at the Sister, aware for the first time that tears were rolling down my cheeks. Gently, she led me away into a small office and went off to find a cup of tea. While she was away, Gerald came by, glancing at me in the office before he went to see the wounded officer for a minute or so. He returned with the Sister.

We drank the tea in silence until I steeled myself to ask Gerald what he thought Gunnar's chances were.

'' Not too good, at present. The blood transfusions have helped a little but severe delayed shock has set in. Doctor Newman feels that the critical time has come—if Gunnar survives the next forty-eight hours then he should be over the worst of the crisis. Who knows ? The human body can take a lot : Gunnar's body has been heavily punished ; he lost so much blood before reaching my RAP''. And then, noticing the anguish on my frozen shocked face, he added gently, '' Remember, if he lives he will be disabled for ever. If he does not, well—you are a Christian like I am. There is little that medicine can do for him now. Let us just say that his life is in God's hands''.

Gerald's words were intended to comfort, yet I felt no lightening of a deep despair. Something told me that I would never see Gunnar again, alive. We had joined the Army together, had been commissioned into the 7th Gurkha Rifles on the same day, had shared so much in the past, and in the future had planned to celebrate a double twenty-first birthday on 20 August, the day between our respective birthdays. Gunnar had an infectious enthusiasm for life, he never sat idle when there was so much to do especially for his beloved Gurkha soldiers who worshipped him, accepting him without any reservations. He was : Hamro (our) Keightly Sahib'.

Keightly was to die two days later without speaking another word. His death hit the Battalion hard because he had been much loved, his loss upset everyone. I withdrew into a cone of silence and grief. In a lonely room, I wrote to my parents for the first time for weeks : the words touched the outer shell of the tragedy without revealing my deep sorrow and guilt.

' Herewith another letter scribbled out in the midst of it all. Life has been quite a party lately—not hectic like the other side (Cassino) must be, but sufficiently lively so as to keep away boredom. I spent over twenty-four hours on a patrol behind—well, almost behind, the German lines. Far too far away from our own men for my liking ! One of my best pals, a lad two days younger than myself, got his leg blown off by a mine that night. Unfortunately three hours elapsed before he reached hospital and the loss of blood was too much—he died. He was unconscious for three days. Only his ' guts' enabled him to survive for so long. A really good boy, an only son. We have lost quite a few killed and wounded ; especially when fighting around Cassino, when it seemed only a matter of time, but no loss has affected me like poor old Keightly's has done'.

The simple stark Military funeral was attended by representatives from all the sub-units in which the dead man had served. The war went on nearby so few men could be spared to pay their last respects. The faltering notes of the bugle aroused me from my silent anguish. As the bugler struggled with the top notes in the the ' Last Post', I heard Gunnar's voice saying in my ear, ' Don't shoot the guy, he's doing his worst'. It was the sort of remark that Gunnar would have made. Then I followed Alan, dropping a little earth into the newly dug grave before saluting smartly. Nothing in the ritual moved me to tears ; I felt we were all taking part in a play entitled '' Gunnar Keightly's Funeral''; the Padre who had officiated at so many of these occasions, the four British officers and the handful of Gurkha soldiers whose impassive Mongolian features hid their feelings about the Christian burial, so different and yet in some respects, so akin to one of their own.

Then I thought about the leading actor, Gunnar Keightly himself. Where had his lively spirit gone ? Snuffed out like a candle or was he alive among the trees and the flowers around me ? I am a Christian, I believe in the life hereafter, I thought. At that moment though the phrase was an empty sounding one. I climbed back into the jeep that was to take me back to the fighting, the war against men who although they spoke another language and still obeyed a maniac called the Fuhrer, nevertheless shared feelings of love and hate, hope and despair, courage and fear, whose young men died of wounds like Gunnar Keightly had done. And many of our opponents were Christians like poor ' Gunnar' had been.

Each Armistice Day I have mourned Keightly, not only as a brother officer who had died before he reached manhood, but because I felt guilty at my failure to help and comfort a dear friend after he had been wounded by the mine.

After bewailing ' poor old Keightly' I tried to give my parents a worm's eye view of the struggle in Italy. ' General Alexander seems to have produced a real trump this time and Gerry must be scratching his head. It isn't finished yet, and he will delay it as long as he can. I expect he will be quite relieved when we have reached the Alps when he can hold many back with a few men'.

Although the German High Command might have been relieved to reach the Alps, Adolph Hitler did not let them abandon any territory in their withdrawal, even if there were tactical reasons for doing so. It was to be fight, fight, all the way until the end of the war. For a young Infantry officer letter writing was never going to be an easy occupation. ' It is hard writing however frequently or infrequently one tries. A lot happens but it is of another world. A life with other values in, the main one being that of fighting. Reading books means only to pass the time away, sport appears to be out of place. I suppose it all adds up to one thing really—our Battalion has a great need of a rest but it is difficult to see when we will be granted one'.

There were other battalions in 4th Indian Division which had been in action for far longer than the 7th Gurkha Rifles. There was not the faintest chance of anyone being relieved. Moreover, many units were being taken from Italy for other assignments. General Alexander's superiority in infantry was marginal, too slender for him to achieve a spectacular victory, even if the German Army's morale had been as low as I felt it was when I wrote, on 12 June : ' The morale of his troops out here is low, very low—not just because he has taken an almighty licking but because he is feeling the hopelessness of it all at last. I give nine months for it to be finished and then back we go to deal with Japan !'

During the summer months of 1944 the Germans continued to retreat, invariably in a planned and controlled manner, buying time in order that the Gothic Line defences, north of Florence and Rimini, could be prepared to meet a major offensive by the Allies, expected in the Autumn. I described what it felt like to be moving after weeks of static warfare. In this instance, the advance was from Lanciano, south of Pescara on the Adriatic front. ' We have been covering quite a bit of ground, visiting en route places which we have looked at from behind cover during the last two months. I was sent with a small party across a river valley, about five miles in width, lying between ridges. It was an amazing experience going through beautiful country and villages but never meeting a living soul, man or animal, on the way. The Eyties however did not take long to come back to their old homes—quite touching to see them staring at their houses, mostly in ruins and battered by war. Life is going to be a struggle for the majority, rebuilding and reorganising their homes and lives again'.

' Taking all in all we had a comparatively easy part to play during these recent operations. The men were bucked when we moved forward as our Gurkhas did not like the static war we have had to wage during the last few weeks. Thank goodness, the weather has been marvellous, making movement a pleasure and not a trial'.

As a postscript to the same letter came a pang of conscience. ' Today, I remembered one thing—your birthday. Is it June or July 8th ? I know I should have remembered which month—anyway my best wishes. Let's hope the next one will have seen this war over'. Fortunately for me, the letter arrived the day before my mother's birthday, which was on 8 July. She forgave me as my letter was, to her, better than any present I could have sent.

I was still alive.

Chapter 3

CHARLIE COMPANY COMMANDER

UNDER Gerry Gordon our Battalion became more professional in outlook. A month out of battle near Campobasso was spent in practising deployment drills, in officers' study days and on training exercises. Reluctantly at first, we came to admit that we had a hell of a lot to learn. In a sense we had been lucky because our deficiences had not been revealed to friend or foe ; our role had invariably been a static one.

Being a junior officer, I did not know whether the rehearsal of deployment technique was solely due to the Colonel's prescience or not. No matter ; it was his enthusiasm that made us realise that there was more to soldiering than killing or being killed. Of equal importance, Gerry Gordon won our confidence and without in any way courting popularity, our affections as well. He was a character and soldiers will follow characters once they are assured that there is a sound leader behind the eccentricities. Colonel Gordon was absent minded and liable to get over excited about comparatively minor details. Although he had but a small band of British officers he invariably called us by the wrong name or forgot what appointment we were holding. Company Commander Trevor Hook and MTO Dougie Crooks became Hookie and Crookie to Gerry Gordon.

One day, he shouted at Hook, OC B Company:

"Crookie, I'd like my jeep today at 1100 hours".

Trevor Hook politely replied : "Fine Sir, but I'm OC 'B' Company".

Gerry in an exasperated tone : "Okay, Crookie—tell Hookie, will you ?"

Those sound judges of British officers, the VCOs (Gurkha officers) admired the Colonel. Like him they were Regulars. At last there was someone training the Battalion like the good 'old days'. They acknowledged that many war-time Sahibs were brave, dashing, keen —but they did not know the real kaida (form). And the Commanding Sahib knew how to 'Ishkeme'. (Scheme in normal English !).

There was talk about using us as high altitude troops which made sense as the Battalion had been trained for such a role during 1943. Several of us were sent on a mountaineering refresher course at

Benevento run by the Americans. The intensive programme of rock-climbing tested nerves and aptitudes. No one from our Battalion failed probably because we knew as much about mountaineering as our instructors. It ended with us feeling outrageously fit. '' Now for a dirty weekend in Rome'', said Matt. Next day we were on the move, driving through Rome and on up to the north. Like Matt, all we could do was to ogle the girls without being given a chance to test our new found fitness and virility.

I need hardly add that another unit was asked to scale the highest mountains, learning their techniques the hard way, while we fought the Germans in the foot hills. Not unique in the annals of war !

Throughout July the Battalion pushed up north from the upper waters of the Rivers Arno and Tiber. It was a hectic time. The advance was rarely easy, subject to delays imposed on us by enemy outposts, minefields, and the occasional counter-attack. It was never easy because the Germans retained the ability to hit back at any time ; life was exciting and exhausting and extreme body fatigue did not encourage us to write letters even if there was a temporary lull. We slept and rested, snatching every possible moment we could before we were off again to seek out the enemy. We lived for the day but for those who waited in England the days without mail were cruel and seemingly without end.

During this period I had no fixed appointment, being used for any stooge job that came up. The Colonel told me that I was the next company commander designate ; I had to wait for one of my friends to be killed or wounded, or the most unlikely but desired alternative, for someone to be rendered ' hors de combat' by natural illness. Meanwhile, the Battalion continued to earn itself a high reputation which was enhanced by ' C' Company when they captured a feature called Campriano.

I will digress because although I played no part in this battle, a Jemadar and a Lance Naik won immediate awards for gallantry during the attack. Both men were called Jitbahadur Rai. His Majesty King George VI watched the battle from an OP so that it was, in every respect, an historic occasion. From that distance his Majesty was not able to see how Lance Naik Jitbahadur Rai won his IDSM. Here is what happened.

Lance Naik Jitbahadur Rai, an ex-mess orderly, undergoing his first experience of battle, was in command of the right hand section. Tracer bullets set fire to some dry grass and, for a moment, the German Spandau fire wavered. Without hesitation the Lance Naik got to his feet and closely followed by the remainder of his section, charged into the wood. Jibahadur was a small man but with two or three swipes of his Kukri he killed two rather obese German gunners who collapsed on top of him. He was therefore under about three hundred and fifty pounds of ' Gerry' when a third gunner came at him. With a supreme effort Jitbahadur got his Kukri arm free and made a blind slash at him, severely wounding the German above the elbow. By this time, Jitbahadur's section had arrived to make the third German a prisoner. It is recorded that Lance Naik Jibahadur was later seen walking alongside the stretcher carrying the prisoner, with a blood stained Kukri in one hand and patting the man's shoulder with the other, reassuring him in fluent Gurkhali that he had no intention of doing anything more now that the wounded man was a prisoner.

Charlie Company with the two Jitbahadurs won high praise for Capriano. Two or three days later, however, their commander, Eric Holton, was evacuated to hospital. To my delight, and surprise, Gerry Gordon told me to take over the company. The CO did not expect Eric to be away for long nor did it seem likely that ' C' Company would be asked to make another major attack before the Battalion withdrew for a rest. Things were going well ; the Battalion's advance was meeting little resistance, the weather was glorious and best of all, I was in command of a Rifle Company.

'' We are the best, Sahib'', the Gurkha officers told me. And they meant it.

It is strange, perhaps, that those four officers are more real to me now than the dozens of Gurkha officers who were to serve with me later, in India, Malaya, Hong Kong, the Borneo territories and the United Kingdom. The senior, Subedar Krishnabahadur Gurung, holds a particular place in my memory because he possessed few of the characteristics one expects to find in a Gurkha. He was thin and wiry, much darker in complexion than his fellows, and was prone to scowls and flashes of temper which did not make him popular with the men. They respected him, admired his courage but feared his sarcastic tongue. A strange man, indeed, and yet in time we became friends.

While Krishnabahadur came from Western Nepal (on transfer from 1/2 Gurkha Rifles), the three platoon commanders (Jemadars) were all from the East. Abidal Limbu was the one who appeared to have the most personality, an extrovert who was always smartly turned out. Although I warmed to him I had heard that he was inclined to talk rather than to act. Is there a better word than bullshit ? I think not. In complete contrast to Abidal was Jemadar Jitbahadur Rai who, as just mentioned, had won a well earned MC. Jitbahadur led his men by example, out in front with no histrionics and no tantrums. He was so dependable, so sound, that there was a natural temptation to give his 9 Platoon the jobs that mattered, the nasty ones. The third Jemadar was a tall slim good looking man, Sherbahadur Sunwar. For some time he appeared to be the weakest of the platoon commanders, probably because he was diffident and inclined to agree with the opinions of the other Gurkha officers. Later, I was to revise my early opinion but by then he had ceased to be under my command.

It says a lot for these officers that my youth and lack of experience did not appear to worry them unduly. Perhaps they did not expect Eric to be away for long and, anyway, they appreciated that it was the turn of the other Rifle companies to be in the van.

Brigadier Hawke now re-enters my story. The open fluid warfare had been much to his liking. The enemy was pulling back affording opportunities for risks and daring tactics. At first all went well but Brigadier Hawke began to overstretch his Brigade, riding his streak of good fortune. I think he was lulled into thinking the Germans would not or could not strike back, a fatal error, and a company of the Cameron Highlanders was to suffer as a result.

Brushing aside the protests of the Commanding officer of the Camerons, Hawke ordered him to send a rifle company to secure a large hill called Monte Grillo. Capturing the lightly held feature was not a big problem. Holding it thereafter, out on a limb without another company being close enough to give any assistance, was inviting a counter stroke. It came. Only one or two men escaped to tell the sad story, to report how after a gallant stand those of their fellows who survived were now prisoners in German hands.

Another company of the Camerons attempted to retake Monte Grillo by the most direct route from the East, but received a bloody nose. Monte Grillo remained in German hands.

We were switched from another sector, in a hurry, to take over from the Camerons—to capture Monte Grillo as quickly as possible. Colonel Gerry Gordon met us, the four rifle company commanders, near an observation post from where we could see our objective. Soon it became obvious that our Colonel had had a vigorous disagreement with the Brigadier. Gerry Gordon had refused to be bulldozed into launching a quick attack. He had insisted on deploying three rifle companies as opposed to sending a single company into yet another piecemeal attack ; he had obtained the Brigadier's reluctant agreement to abandoning a direct assault, in favour of a long approach march of three miles across undulating, uncharted country, towards our objective, Monte Grillo.

Monte Grillo was a bastion of the great Prato Magno Alps. It was like a giant dumbbell, falling away steeply on all sides except at the northern end where there was a gradual descent through a thick forest. Then followed half a mile of heather and boulders, after which the ground rose steeply to a peak, surmounted by the old ruined castle of Monte Acuto.

Time was needed for careful reconnaissance by all officers and

NCOs ; by putting back the attack twenty four hours the Colonel ensured that this was possible. From the observation posts we gazed across the valley at Monte Grillo. Indeed, the whole of our objective was clearly visible, scanned from end to end by numerous binoculars, but the undulating countryside could not be seen from our vantage point. Gerry Gordon was taking a calculated risk that the Germans would not be expecting an attack from this flank especially after such a long and difficult cross-country approach. Fortunately for us, his appreciation was sound : '' The Commanding Sahib's scheme is a good one'', was the unanimous opinion of my Gurkha officers. I agreed.

All the Intelligence indicated that the main German position was on the eastern end of Monte Grillo which B Company was to seize. C Company's objective was on the left flank, which the Colonel expected to be the easiest one for the most junior of his company commanders. I was happy with our role being under no illusions about my lack of experience in commanding men in a major battle.

The Camerons had attacked from the East. We attacked from the south-west with a smoke deception plan being fired against the eastern slopes of Monte Grillo. Faced with an approach march of three miles the assaulting rifle companies set of at 1930 hours, 6 August, with their final assault being scheduled for 0300 hours next morning. I cannot say how B and D companies fared during the march ; as far as I was concerned it was a harrowing experience, caused not by the enemy but by our, or my, inability to keep going in the right direction.

In daylight it had seemed so easy with Monte Grillo in clear view on the other side of the valley. Every NCO had been shown the route from the OP with the sun shining and pinpointing the various landmarks, making them easy to identify on the map and on the ground. Now it was a dark night and after we descended into the valley, nothing seemed to be the same. The leading platoon under Jemadar Abidal Limbu set out full of confidence and kept going for about half an hour. Then they began to hesitate, stopping, starting, and then stopping again. Eventually a runner came out of the night to whisper, '' Sahib, Jemadar Sahib wishes to speak with you''.

I followed him past a long line of Gurkha riflemen who were patiently squatting on their haunches in a way few Europeans can find relaxation. At the head of the snake-like column I met Abidal : in a most cheerful whisper, he happily told me that he was lost. In all honesty I was not surprised because our objective had not been visible for some time, which made me feel some alarm. Of more importance, I had not been checking our direction on my compass. In my inexperience I had assumed that Abidal and his NCOs would lead us to the ' Start Line'. It was a lesson I never forgot but it was hardly the time to be learning my trade as a company commander.

Subedar Krishnabahadur Gurung joined us. Compass bearings were taken, maps opened and consulted on the ground using shaded torches, and opinions sought and exchanged. I had no idea where we were and would have accepted advice from the most junior member of the company if he had given it with verve and confidence. Abidal and Krishnabahadur had different opinions, which made it even more difficult. Swayed by the Subedar's seniority, I inclined to his views— and off we went in another direction.

An hour later after many frustrating halts, conferences, stops and starts, it was distressingly clear that we had been going round in a circle. By this time the men were tired, loudly grumbling, and I was near to tears. I realised that the time had come for me to assert lost authority, to stop the aimless wandering around. My watch told me that it was well after midnight. Allied artillery was due to begin firing a pre-planned programme against Monte Grillo at 0200 hours, one hour before our assault began. Right, I said, we will stay where we are until the guns open up. That will show us where our objective is—then we will move like the wind, doubling most of the way if necessary.

To Subedar Krishnabahadur Gurung it was a horrifying decision, an admission of defeat. Charlie Company never got lost and, he added, what would B and D Company say if we failed to guard their left flank and did not cross the start line when they did ? He was furious when I stood my ground : for a moment I had a horrible feeling that he was going to be mutinous and order the men to follow him. He did not, contenting himself with a few muttered curses before he sat down, away from me, and sulked in silence while we waited until 0200 hours. It was a hell of a long wait. At the time I felt ashamed of my incompetence, but in retrospect, it was a sensible decision to sit and wait.

Just before 0200 hours, the platoon commanders ensured that all the men were ready to move as soon as the guns began firing. We peered at our watches and then, at last, heard the thunder of the artillery as it opened up behind us. A few seconds later there was the crump crump and flashes of the shells as they landed—Abidal had been right, Monte Grillo was further to our left. Our early disagreement seemed quite unimportant when we saw how far the objective was from where we had been waiting. Krishnabahadur agreed that it would be wise for us to run while out of earshot of the enemy and this we did, doubling with some difficulty, encumbered by rucksacks and weapons including small mortars and bombs.

After making the best speed possible for about half a mile, Monte Grillo was revealed before us, looming high above our heads. Our guns continued to fire their programme of hate against the enemy positions ; a glance at my watch showed that there were another fifteen minutes before we were due to cross the assault ' start line' at the foot of the hill. Around me, the company was in complete disarray, with the stronger, fitter men to the fore and their weaker brethren in the rear struggling hard to keep up. All were breathless and exhausted. I managed to stop the leading group, then told the platoon commanders to regain control of their men. I realised that we had to go into the attack as an organised company, and not as an exhausted band of cross country runners, unable to battle with an alert foe.

Once again Subedar Krishnabahadur became most agitated ; he was unduly sensitive about the ribbing he might receive from the Gurkha officers of the other companies if C Company should fail to attack the enemy at the appointed ' zero hour'. I brooked no interference, however, from the Subedar, telling him sharply that as soon as he reported that the three platoons were complete, then we would be off.

Three or four minutes later, we were shaking ourselves out into open formation, walking quickly but without actually breaking into another tiring, shambling run. At five minutes to three, the Allied artillery stopped firing on Monte Grillo, to begin engaging targets to the north behind the hill : we were about three hundred yards from our ' start line' when loud shouts of ' Charge, Ayo Gurkhali' were heard on our right.

It was B or D company, or both, going into the attack. Subedar Krishnabahadur said : " I told you so, Sahib, we are late".

We were, but it was not to matter. The Germans were flabbergasted at the direction of our attack ; complete surprise was attained and the initial fight for possession of Monte Grillo did not take long.

My men went up the hill shouting in excitement which was understandable after a march that had taken over seven hours. A few shots were fired at the right hand men of 7 platoon, which gave them an excuse to go roaring in, chanting the traditional bloodcurdling 'Ayo Gurkhali' before they reached the crest—only to find that the ' Dushmen' had fled.

For a couple of minutes I was as excited and elated as the most junior rifleman in the company. It was a glorious moment, one to be savoured. We stood around chatting as if the war was over.

Fortunately the sarcastic tongued Subedar appeared out of the night to chastise the men, cursing them for sitting around when they ought to be digging.

" The dushman' will come, and so will his mortars, and you, my children, will all be dead unless you do something about it".

His medicine worked. Ashamedly following his advice, I gave 7 and

9 Platoons areas of responsibility below the crest of the hill. We left them digging and preparing their positions and went down to site the reserve platoon, under Jemedar Sherbahadur Sunwar, close to our Company Headquarters.

Just as we had reached the bottom of the hill all hell was let loose. Firing, shouting, screaming and confusion reigned. Subedar Krishnabahadur thought that the right hand 7 Platoon, under Abidal Limbu, was being attacked. Together we set off up the hill. In the early glimmerings of dawn men appeared running towards us. Three or four brushed us aside while others stopped when my Subedar, brandishing his tommy gun, threatened to shoot the lot of them. Excitedly at first but gradually calming down, they said that their platoon position had been overrun and the Germans were there in force, occupying the crest of the ridge. " Where then is your platoon commander ?'' spat out Subedar Krishnahabadur.

They hung their heads in shame. We turned them round and slowly, tactically, we went back up the hill. By now all was quiet. A few yards below the top, still on the rear slopes, we found Abidal and one section of his men. His story was that a strong fighting patrol had approached to within a few yards, gone to ground and then hurled dozens of stick grenades at 7 Platoon. Before the Jemedar could give out any orders more than half his men had taken to their heels and run.

Those men that had returned with us went back to their positions and dug. During the next five days they fought as well as they had ever fought before or were to do thereafter. Never again did I see the handful who had fled into the night. Subedar Krishnabahadur Gurung sent word back to B Echelon that they were not to be there when he returned with the Company after the current action was over. I did not find out what happened to them. Our four Gurkha officers spat on the ground in disgust whenever the incident was mentioned in the Company. I suspect that they never told the other rifle companies; it was a blot Charlie Company wished to forget.

Later, years later, I began to understand why they had fled. I had learnt by then that Gurkhas are not supermen : lack of sleep added to nervous tension and confusion will make them react in the same way as soldiers from other nations have done since war between men started. And one single frightened man can spread fear like a common infection.

The Germans, having probed our defences with some success, had withdrawn. I wonder if they appreciated how near to victory they had been ? And it would not have been the first time during the Italian campaign that a quick enemy thrust, a local counter attack delivered before the assaulting troops could reorganise, was to win back a position with comparative ease.

I was a shaken young man because I realised how near to a disaster it had been. Never again would I have been allowed to command a company in action. I would have been posted away, my whole life and career would have been changed if the spontaneous scuttle of men had spread to the other platoons. Certainly I would not have chosen the army as a career at the end of the war nor would my superiors have recommended me for a Regular commission if I had done so. On such slender threads do our lives depend.

Right, I thought, the soldiers of 7 Platoon are shaky so I will stay here alongside Jemedar Abidal until they regain their self confidence. Subedar Krishnabahadur remonstrated but not with any conviction, because he, too, had been unsettled by events, still angry and metaphorically spitting with rage. I felt it would be better if he went back to organise company headquarters and virtually act as company commander until I deemed it wise to go back and join him.

Dawn was fast approaching. There was so much to be done before full daylight came. The riflemen needed no reminding that foxholes and weapon pits had to be scratched out of the earth and rocks if they were going to survive. They set to with gusto while I went from post to post joking with them, trying hard to appear nonchalant as well as showing them that I forgave those who had panicked but had returned to fight. We stopped at first light, the traditional time for assaults in war as well as in peacetime exercises, and lay on the ground or took up positions in half dug pits to watch, to listen. After about five minutes the Germans showed their appreciation of our ' stand to ' by bringing down an accurate mortar strike, then they hurled a few stick grenades which came over the crest of the hill. One of my sections began firing indiscriminately for no purpose whatever. I rushed across, oblivious to bomb and grenades, shouting at them to hold their fire because ammunition would be needed later. They did so. One young rifleman seized me by the arm and pulled me down behind a half completed shelter where we huddled like squashed tomatoes. When I had recovered my breath, he told me with a broad smile that I was a brave Sahib to risk mortars but I would soon die if I continued to wander round in the open. His remarks met with the approval of his mates in the section. His simple praise, spoken with affection. made me happy. I had begun to be accepted by some of the men in C Company.

When the dose of hate had ended, we counted heads. Everyone had stood firm but regrettably there was a handful of casualties. The tension and excitement of the long night left me desperately tired and depressed. However, Abidal was being his cheerful self again, organising the evacuation of the wounded, urging the able bodied to greater efforts in the preparation of their positions. For the moment I was superfluous and for reasons I cannot analyse now, dearly wanted to be reassured in my own tongue, English. The lull in the battle enabled me to walk across to D Company on our right, with my purpose being to liaise with Tim Brown, the company commander.

We met, conveniently for me, at his left hand platoon which was not far from Abidal's men. Tim was surprisingly jaunty, elated and quite unruffled. Just talking with him was a tonic which I needed because I had not recovered from the shock of our mini-retreat. Pride in C Company stopped me from giving him any details nor did he ask questions. Instead we discussed the problem that faced our three rifle companies on Monte Grillo : only now did we appreciate how big the mountain was. In the morning light it was like an immense dumb bell and the Germans still held the northern end. The mountain overlooked the Arno valley below, and dominated the only road leading into the Prato Magno Alps. It was a place of vital importance which the Germans decided they would not give up without a fierce struggle : their decision to remain and fight it out meant that the Battalion was fully extended for the next three days and nights.

During that first day on Monte Grillo I had the last of my clashes with Subedar Krishnabahadur Gurung. Or perhaps more accurately it should be termed a disagreement because there was little rancour on either side. In retrospect, I realised he was right and I was wrong. After returning to 7 Platoon I instructed Jemadar Abidal to make some adjustments in his position which, in turn, meant moving the left hand 9 Platoon under Jemadar Jitbahadur Rai. The riflemen of both platoons accepted these changes stoically, even though it meant many of them abandoning half-dug positions and having to start the back-breaking task of building new weapon pits from scratch once more.

So far, so good. My presence earlier that morning had helped the men of 7 Platoon recover their confidence. The liaison visit to D Company had revealed a dangerous gap between us which was now in the process of being closed ; against our new look, well prepared defences, it would be difficult for the Germans to win back the left sector of the Monte Grillo feature without a mighty effort, costly in lives and supporting fire. But my task with the forward platoon was over and it was time to move back to Company Headquarters at the foot of the rear slopes. So said Subedar Krishnabahadur, when he came forward to find out how we were faring.

He was right to press me but he pleaded in vain. Stubbornly refusing to accept his advice, I remained with 7 Platoon Headquarters. Our argument did not last long because, I believe, the Subedar had heard from Abidal and his soldiers that the ' Sanu Sahib' (junior officer) had inspired them at a crucial stage. Nevertheless, as Krishnabahadur pointed out, that was in the past and it would be impossible for me to command the Company from a foxhole just below the crest, away from direct radio and telephone communications with Battalion Headquarters. Fortunately the Germans decided to ram such a lesson quietly down my throat without making C Company pay for the folly of their inexperienced commander. An enemy fighting patrol tried to work round our open left flank, supported by a liberal bombardment from their mortars. Subedar Krishnabahadur co-ordinated the counteraction, ranged artillery fire against the German intruders, and ordered the reserve platoon into a blocking position, while I was unable to move back to join him because of the mortar bombardment, listening in on the 7 Platoon radio to the Subedar as he did my job for me—most efficiently.

Half an hour later a chastened but wiser British officer arrived at Company headquarters to be greeted with genuine relief by Subedar Krishnabahadur Gurung. For a man not renowned for his tact it was surprising that he refrained from claiming in public a moral victory over his young commander—perhaps his forbearance, more than anything else, cemented the deep feelings of trust and affection that grew up between us. Krishnabahadur had few friends among the British and Gurkha officers and, after the war, I often found myself his sole defender. Those who assailed him in peace had not witnessed his courage, loyalty and tenacity in tight corners, qualities which were all too quickly forgotten by many after the fighting was over.

Ours was but a minor clash compared with the one that unseated our Commanding Officer, Gerry Gordon. All my facts have been gained at second or third hand but the ending is true, even if some of the details have been tinged with fiction over the years.

When Brigadier Hawke heard about the light casualty figures we had incurred while capturing Monte Grillo, his reaction was to say that the bulk of the enemy must have pulled back, otherwise the prize would have exacted a much heavier toll in lives. In saying this he was completely wrong. Gerry Gordon had outwitted the defenders who had fled in surprise ; thereafter they had shown all too clearly that they had no intention of giving up Monte Grillo without a hell of a fight. The Brigadier's attitude infuriated Gerry Gordon but unfortunately there was more to come. Hawke decided that the Germans must not be allowed to recover their poise and balance, that the time had come to exploit their difficulties and open up a way to the town of Bibbiena, in the north. Denis Dougall, who had recently taken over adjutant, was called to the radio. The Brigade-Major told him that one of the three rifle companies on Monte Grillo was to move at once to capture another feature, a mile or two to the north. The timing of the order could not have been worse as it coincided with the German probing attack around C Company's left flank. Gerry Gordon was sitting near the other radio, listening to Subedar Krishnabahadur Gurung who was controlling the battle from my headquarters. In the usual fog of war, confusion, excitement and exaggeration, it appeared at that time as if it was a major attempt by the enemy to get behind C Company and then cut us off. The Colonel was co-ordinating the artillery fire plan with a gunner officer when Dougall gave him the latest order from Brigade Headquarters. The Colonel exploded. Legend has it that his first words were :

"Tell him to stuff it—and tell him there's a war on here".

Dougall duly passed on the Colonel's message albeit in a more polite form. A minute or two later he came back to tell Gerry that the Brigade Sunray (the Brigadier) wanted him to go back to Brigade Headquarters at once—to discuss the order. In fury, the Colonel charged at the wireless set and grabbed the microphone linking him with Brigade HQ. Battalion folk lore has it that he said : "Tell your f - - - - - g Sunray that if he wishes to speak to me he can bloody well come here. Tell him there's a f - - - - - g war on. Out". Whether these words have been correctly recorded or not, matters little. Colonel Gerry Gordon meant what he said and, of course, he had right on his side. It is a well tried maxim of war that in an emergency, the senior commander goes forward to consult his juniors, to seek out information, to advise and give firm instructions. The 7th Gurkhas was being attacked and it was wrong for the Commanding Officer to have been given an order to leave his post of duty at that time. The fact that the German attack later proved to be a probing one only does not change the situation one little bit.

Gerry Gordon was sacked. The three rifle companies on Monte Grille knew nothing about this clash of personalities until, at the end of the day a short message was received over the field telephone to say that Desmond had taken over command, once more. At the time we assumed that Colonel Gerry Gordon was sick and would be away a matter of hours or possibly days at the most : later when the full story was known, when we knew that he would never return, the astonishment and disbelief shown by the Gurkha officers was testimony to their feelings for our ex Commanding Officer. To them and to all of us it was quite incredible that the Commanding Sahib should be removed at the height of a most efficiently organised battalion attack, one that cost few lives but had won an important victory by surprise. It was a sad moment for us and a bitter blow for Gerry Gordon.

Our ex Commanding Officer's act of defiance did, however, suspend any further movement forward from Monte Grillo. The Brigadier changed his mind even if he did not forgive Gerry Gordon. Meanwhile we stayed on Monte Grillo for three days and nights, and were given no rest by the Germans. The hot August weather added to our discomfort, water being especially short as it had to be carried forward from behind and this often proved impossible during the daylight hours. With Subedar Krishnabahadur by my side I began to learn how to command a company of soldiers. If I had been a sub-altern in a British unit then I would have graduated from being a platoon commander to company second-in-command ; only in an emergency or after heavy casualties, would I have ever commanded a company. In a Gurkha battalion it was different. British officers com-manded companies, the Gurkha officers (Viceroy's commissioned officers) filled nearly all the other appointments. Apprenticeship I had none before being given the heavy responsibility of commanding about a hundred men in action.

With the Subedar's support I managed to cope but only because C Company had a static role during those three days on Monte Grillo. If we had up-sticks, advanced, and had to co-operate with armour or had been asked to carry out a more difficult operation of war, then my shortcomings as a company commander would have been all too obvious.

After he had persuaded me to base myself at the nodal point of C Company affairs, company headquarters, Krishnabahadur devoted himself to curbing my enthusiastic efforts to do everything myself. After twenty-four hours of maximum activity my body began to flag, my mind to wander. I had to rest. I realised later that while I slept, affairs had been run efficiently by the Subedar—so, perhaps, I was not indispensable after all ? Tactfully my mentor pressed home the point, there was a staff at company headquarters, each man had his own role to play ; slowly I began to realise what tasks to decentralise and what I had to carry out myself. With my keenness to learn being so apparent, the Subedar's tough attitude softened until, in time, he took pride in the way I was learning my trade as a company com-mander.

For three days and nights a stalemate existed on Monte Grillo. The Germans showed no signs of withdrawing from positions on the opposite slopes below the crest, while our three companies were equally well ensconced and dug in on the rear slopes of the hill. But whenever our patrols probed forward after dark they encountered enemy fire as soon as they crossed the skyline. At the time it seemed as if we were to be locked in close combat for many days to come. I spent much of my time calling for artillery and mortar support, then correcting the fire when our observation posts sent back reports. On the other side of the hill my opposite number was doing the same. I suspect that he did it better than I did if results were to be judged by the accuracy of his mortar strikes against C Company's defences.

So far I have made no mention of casualties ; fortunately we suffered fewer than was to be expected chiefly because the men dug and dug until most positions could withstand anything except a direct hit.

Our stretcher bearers were magnificent : nothing seemed to daunt them after a cry for help had been received from a forward platoon. Out into the open would charge two men, occasionally ducking or throwing themselves flat when a shell landed nearby, but never being diverted for long from their mission of mercy. Rough and tough though these young lads were, they were transformed when a wounded man was in their charge. Their gentleness and compassion was surprisingly feminine which seemed out of character. Indeed, back in the Lebanon in 1943 Doc Sausman had complained bitterly that the men who had been sent to him to be trained as stretcher bearers were ' thugs', he accused company Gurkha officers of having selected big strong men without any brains for duties that required intelligence. In a sense he was right because the Gurkha officers were influenced by misguided motives ; in practice, however, he was quick to admit that although they were slow to learn his stretcher bearers never forgot his teaching nor did they ever shirk danger or discomfort. Nowadays Gurkha soldiers are comparatively well educated and can read and write, and many speak English. In 1944 the opposite was true ; even the senior NCOs had little education because promotion was so quick in war time. This meant that the company commander in action found himself doing many tasks that would be done by junior NCOs now—purely because he, alone, could read English.

So it was on the medical side : all casualties were brought back to Company HQ before being evacuated to the Battalion Aid Post. I found myself acting as assistant medical orderly, injecting morphia and interpreting English instructions on phials and labels.

The fighting at Cassino had taught me to steel myself to look at ghastly wounds without feeling faint or involuntarily showing revulsion. I learnt to detach myself to a certain extent. Or did I ? I wonder, especially when I remember the fatalistic bearing of the mortally wounded men as they waited uncomplainingly for evacuation or slowly died in pain while we watched, powerless to alleviate their suffering, their brown eyes gazing at us in trust or fear. In complete contrast, many of the lightly wounded men made a great fuss about their injuries, rolling their eyes, monotonously saying ''ai-ya,ai-ya''. Such reflections are not based on the Second World War alone ; later in Malaya and then in Borneo the same pattern seemed to persist, with lightly wounded soldiers quick to indulge in public displays of self pity.

On the third day at the height of a mortar strike, Denis Dougall spoke to me on the field telephone. Good news, he said, 2/4 Gurkha Rifles from 10 Division is going to relieve the Battalion during the night. He went on to say that two of their companies would move into B and D positions on my right—a strong patrol only would occupy our C Company position.

When I told my Gurkha officers that our position on the left was considered to be the least important of the three, they had somewhat pungent comments to make. With good reason : after the first day, the pressure against the other two companies had decreased and switched onto our sector. The Germans sensed that if they could get round the open flank, on our left, then they would roll up the whole of the battalion position.

I remonstrated with my Colonel, Desmond. The Commanding Officer of 2/4 GR had made the decision. It was his battalion that would be fighting the battle after midnight, and my fears were considered to be unjustified. Later, outside the company headquarters dugout, the sun shone and all was quiet for the first time for many hours. Perhaps I was wrong, perhaps CO 2/4 GR was right ? For a few moments I sunbathed but found it too hot. I moved to some shade near a broken wall and sat down. With no military purpose in my mind I was idly scanning a clump of trees on our left. To my astonishment, in the lens of my binoculars, almost as if he was within touching distance, there was a German officer dressed in grey. He was at the end of the wood ; he was looking at me through binoculars. For a second or two I thought I was imagining things. I lowered my binoculars in disbelief then looked again. There he was. We continued to gaze at each other. I was stunned with amazement and then he raised his hand in a mock Nazi salute before turning back into the trees.

I doubled back to the wireless and called for our guns to fire onto the wood. It was a pre-arranged target. My conscience dictated that I took some action against the enemy, but secretly I hoped the brave impudent soul escaped. Subedar Krishnabahadur was annoyed that I had not fired my rifle at him. I confess that my initial shock at seeing him so close to our position had put such a thought out of my mind.

When I reported the incident to Desmond by telephone, he warned us to be on our guard. The German officer would have an accurate idea of the company layout and dispositions. Later he rang back to say that after discussing the sighting with his opposite number, the Colonel of the 4th Gurkhas, the latter had decided that C Company would be the last company to move back : originally we had been scheduled to move first as soon as the patrol from 2/4 GR had arrived, followed by B and D companies of the battalion in that order.

The caution of the two colonels was justified by events that evening. I had completed an inspection tour of the whole Company position after dark and had reached my headquarters when the German attack began. The ' peeping tom' of the morning had not wasted his time. 7 and 9 Platoons were kept at full stretch by a series of raids during which showers of stick grenades descended on and among their weapon pits. My men fought magnificently. The Germans tried rushing one post then another. On one occasion they were met half way by four Gurkhas under a Lance Naik. With drawn kukries they charged at the enemy who fled over the crest of the hill while the section commander, had to physically restrain his men from chasing after the fleeing figures.

The crisis was not over, however, as 8 Platoon and Company head-quarters were battered by heavy mortaring, most accurately pin-pointed on our positions at the foot of the rear slopes—more evidence of our friend's daring reconnaissance. His idea had been to drive a wedge between the two forward platoons while we in the rear were pinned down by mortars, unable to help. It did not succeed but it was the courage and tenacity of 7 and 9 Platoons who won not one battle but several because the Germans would withdraw, pause, then strike again.

Long before midnight I had recommended that my company should not be relieved that night—even if 2/4 GR had a complete company to take over our positions, a relief in the line would have been a tricky if not impossible operation. At a quarter to twelve, Alan Howard told me that our B and D companies had been relieved as planned and had withdrawn without any interference from the enemy. Colonel 2/4 GR was now my new boss—for the next twenty-four hours anyway. He wished me luck. Thereafter unfamiliar voices on the radio and field telephone spoke to us—our friends were on their way back to rest, to safety, and — glory be — to the luxury of a hot bath !

Shortly afterwards the Germans gave up and desisted from any further attacks. I went round the company positions, from section to section, post to post, congratulating the men. '' When are we being relieved ?'' they asked. When I told them we were staying for another twenty-four hours they accepted the news in a resigned manner. They could not understand why 2/4 GR could not relieve us before dawn especially as there were at least four hours of darkness left. I pointed out that it was too late to change the original plan but as I made my way back to company headquarters, I had to admit that I could have asked for a temporary postponement rather than a complete twenty-four hour delay in our relief. Soon I was to realise that I was the only person in the whole company who was keen to stay on Monte Grillo. Why, I asked myself, many years later ? The answer, a confession, is that I did not expect to be given the chance to command a company again. I thought that some personal kudos would be obtained if C Company had to spend an extra day and night in action. Fortunately these thoughts were not passed on to any of the Gurkha officers or men : quite rightly they would not have shared my immature and naive desire for glory !

As true professionals they were prepared to fight at any time but this did not mean volunteering for an extra twenty-four hours under shell, bomb and bullet when the rest of the battalion were relaxing, miles away from the front line.

I would be guilty of invention if I was to describe what occurred during the daylight hours of our fourth day on the Monte Grillo feature. My rag-bag of memories is bare. Recently in frustration I turned to the official history of the 7th Gurkha Rifles—nothing except one sentence to the effect that C Company remained behind under 2/4 GR for another day. So, to the 4th Gurkha Rifles history, to find that their historian had forgot to mention that C Company 2/7 GR battled on for an extra day. Obviously therefore the lack of recollections means that we must have had a peaceful time. The only point that I recorded afterwards was that all ranks of C Company kept their heads well down throughout the extra spell in the front line which, unbeknown to them, was earned by their temporary commander's enthusiasm—not an unworthy motive—and his desire to snatch a few more hours in the driving seat—a deplorable piece of immaturity, I confess.

What I did do was to ask if we could be relieved as soon as it was dark, and short of a major assault being launched that, this time, there would be no postponement. Assurances were given and at the appointed hour, men from the 4th Gurkha Rifles came in, platoon by platoon, section by section, to take over our defences. The relief in the line went with remarkable smoothness because the Germans co-operated by leaving our sector alone. When I reported on the phone that the change over had been completed, the Intelligence officer of the 2/4 Gurkha Rifles asked me to call in at their headquarters to meet his Colonel. He would arrange for my jeep to be standing by near the headquarters so that Subedar Krishnabahadur Gurung could take the company away in the other transport without waiting for me.

Accompanied by my faithful friend and watch dog, Rifleman Rambahadur, I walked up the track to the farm which housed 2/4 GR's headquarters. Away behind us I could hear the faint noise of the trucks which were taking the company away to Lake Trasimeno. We were greeted with enthusiastic warmth by everyone in the house and especially by their Commanding Officer. He was not to know my real motives for volunteering to stay behind another day; on the contrary, he expressed the opinion that if C Company had not re-mained then the Germans would have infiltrated in from the left and cut off his two rifle companies. Before my first whisky I felt like an imposter; after my second, I was sure that we had saved the newly arrived, inexperienced battalion from suffering a real disaster! I ought to explain that during our stay in the front line I had refused to drink any alcohol. Such temporary abstinence was self-imposed. Our battalion had one or two heavy drinkers among the British officers' cadre and I had seen how alcohol had made them careless and rash on more than one occasion—hence my caution, my refusal to touch drink on Monte Grillo.

The whiskies given to us by our hosts went straight down into empty stomachs and rocked nervous systems stretched by tension and a grave shortage of sleep. For many reasons we were intoxicated when on departure we shook hands all round ; outside in the night we came to a mutual agreement that we were drunk and moreover appeared to be incapable of finding our jeep. We went in the wrong direction. I insisted on taking a compass bearing which reduced Rambahadur to helplessness under a fit of giggles. I assured him that I was not only the senior but also the more sober of the two inebriated men. Recalling our walk through Cassino town at night, I remember saying : " We will go that way—and I will lead". Rambahadur sat on the ground doubled up with laughter which sobered me enough to realise we were making a hell of a noise near someone else's battle-field. Whether we would have found our jeep that night by our own efforts is debatable. Our saviour was the jeep driver who, tired of waiting, had walked towards the farm. He heard our laughter and came to find us. He was not amused.

As soon as the jeep reached the main road Rambahadur was fast asleep. I was too excited and, it must be written, proud of what C Company had achieved under my leadership. How quickly we forget our mistakes and fears, and mercifully too, the nasty, unpleasant things of life.

The Battalion had moved back to a delightful area beside the beauti-ful Lake Trasimeno. Subedar Krishnabahadur's convoy had arrived about an hour before the jeep driver delivered his two tired and none too coherent passengers. The first person to greet me was Eric Holton, the ' real' Company Commander, restored to health and re-instated from the moment I met him. It would be stupid to claim that I was surprised but it would be dishonest to deny that I was deeply disappointed. Eric was in his late twenties and whatever I had or had not achieved, he was the appointed commander of Charlie Company.

Being a generous friendly man, Eric went out of his way to make me feel wanted by the Company. He asked Desmond if I could remain as company officer but this was turned down for reasons which will be apparent in the next chapter. Krishnabahadur insisted on me being guest of honour at the company nautch (celebration/dance) that was going to be held the following night, an honour that rarely comes to a subaltern.

Those readers, who have attended similar functions in the British Army's Brigade of Gurkhas after 1948, will have a different conception of a Gurkha nautch. Let me say straight away that our war-time celebrations were spontaneous, boasted no sophisticated aids like stages, costumes, high-fi apparatus, nor was there any Indian orientated music or dances. At Lake Trasimeno the men of C Company sat in a gigantic circle under the light provided by a friendly moon. At the start the British and Gurkha officers sat on chairs in a small group but it was not long before we were being coerced, some-times physically, into displaying our clumsy talents as dancers—to the friendly catcalls of the riflemen. Or we sat on the ground sur-rounded by a group of men who wanted to forget the war or that you were an officer or that Subedar Krishnabahadur could be a sarcastic bastard. It was on such a night that I really understood that men truly can be brothers, that in war we have a deep love for those who have shared danger and overcome the same fears ; that the 7th Gurkha Rifles was the best regiment of all ; and C Company was streets ahead of the other companies in the battalion. The heady mix-ture of potent rum added to my relief at being alive was made com-plete by the exciting, throbbing madals (drums), and the soldier ' dancers' whose faces gleamed with sweat, their masculine squat bodies moving with a feminine grace. Their expressions showed that thoughts were miles away, back in the hills of Nepal even though they were busily entertaining friends by the shore of Lake Trasimeno.

When or how we ended that nautch, I cannot remember, nor is it relevant to the story. What I can recall was an impromptu speech by Jemadar Abidal Limbu to those who had kept the party going until dawn was breaking. He ended up by saying that 'Our Lieutenant Smith Sahib belongs to Charlie Company. He is now our Sahib and we want him to command us again'. Eric applauded as loudly as anyone. I wanted to reply, but could not. I was drunk, not with the rum I had consumed but overcome by deep emotion. The tears in my eyes were for real ; I cried because I had been accepted as an equal by the best company in the British Army.

What more could a young subaltern want from life ? Nothing, then, except a good long sleep !

Next day I wrote an overdue letter to my patient, long-suffering parents : "At last I have found time, peace and the spirit suitable for writing letters. I expect you have been quite worried over the lack of mail in the last month—however, you are an old soldier and realise that three or four weeks will often pass before my mail becomes regular and frequent".

These words were addressed to my Mother. Although each letter started with the words, " Dear Mum and Dad", the ties of love and affection were with my mother : my father was a shy man of few words who never wrote. Between us there was a mutual respect but our relationship was never a close one. And so, at Lake Trasimeno, I celebrated my 21st Birthday at peace. It meant little to me as the memory of the absent guest, Gunnar Keightly, was a heavy burden on my conscience. Somehow it was an anti-climax, so that I did not mention my birthday until the evening. It seemed the best way to remember my friend—quietly, without a party.

Chapter 4

TAVOLETO

ONCE again the Battalion had to readjust its ways to another CO, or, more,accurately, had to remember what life was like under Desmond when he last commanded us, some three months before. It was quite a change : more relaxed and easy going, less tension but a trifle chaotic was my opinion. Desmond liked being one of ' the boys' which in a sense, he was, being still under thirty years of age. Compared with Gerry Gordon he was a gay amateur who tried to hide his lack of experience behind a full measure of Irish charm, blarney and banter.

I was too serious minded a young man, and probably too much of a prude, to have an easy relationship with Desmond. I liked him, envied his happy go lucky manner but never did I feel that he was competent enough to be commanding a battalion in action. Now, years later, I am sure that he was fortunate in having an experienced team of British company commanders and senior Gurkha VCOs. My verdict is that he was no more fitted to command a battalion than I was a rifle company but both of us did our best !

The few days spent beside Lake Trasimeno were idyllic, peaceful and relaxing. For those who had spent many weeks at the sharp end, there was the reward of a short holiday in Rome ; officially termed ' rest and relaxation' this leave was retitled ' sex and fornication' by our joker, Matt Mulloy. He set off to put words into deeds and returned full of stories that became more colourful each time Matt recounted them to an audience generous with their laughter, eager to be amused. I did not qualify for R and R or S and F, it did not worry me unduly—I would have been frightened stiff by those Roman maidens if only half Matt's stories were authentic.

Even without leave, my morale was high. I wrote of my feelings for the Gurkhas I had led in battle, words that were tinged with emotion : ''Our battalion is becoming a first class one and with more experience, we hope to emulate the others in 4th Indian Division. Gurkhas are terrific in attack and are usually given the toughest nut to crack. Considering that they come from a country which is not in the Empire, do not know who or what Hitler is, or even care, their spirit and willingness to fight for the British is incredible''.

I was not the first or last British officer to be moved to write in such terms about his beloved Gurkha soldiers. Soon they, and I, were going to be tested again because the battles for the Gothic Line were to be launched on 1st September, 1944.

It is unfortunate that I was unable to write another letter during the next three weeks. I was not to know then that the most incident-packed days of my life were to occur during the last week in August and the first three days of September. It is not surprising that nothing was recorded but it is a pity. All I can do is to summarise what happened before I was able to resume writing letters to my parents.

The peace and quiet beside Lake Trasimeno was of a short duration which did not surprise the officers and men of the 4th Indian Division. Visits by senior officers who were generous with praise about our past deeds and always ready to exhort all ranks to greater efforts in the future, meant that something big was being planned. Then came the large, bluff ex-Guardsman who had the unenviable task of following Monty as Eighth Army Commander. Wisely he did not attempt to ape his illustrious predecessor ; indeed, it was to his credit that he behaved like a cheerful Guards office —which he was. Afterwards I recorded that the General's visit bordered on farce, the worthy man emerging as a figure of fun rather than as a leader inspiring us to deeds of valour.

All British and Gurkha officers present stood in a line to meet the Army Commander. Slowly he moved down, starting from the Battalion second-in-command. Soon it became obvious that the General had two standard questions ; what is your name and how long have you been doing your present job ? Irrespective as to whether the answer to the second question was six months or six days, the General's reply was, '' Good show, good show'', before he moved on to the next officer. The Gurkha officers were being subjected to the same ' good show' treatment when the unfortunate man had to retreat at a lively trot to the nearest field latrine.

An erratic stomach complaint had led to his undignified withdrawal. Behind the hessian screen, sitting on the adjacent seat of the mobile ' loo', the Army Commander found the Battalion second-in-command, who after receiving his own ' good show' had made a dash for the same reason. The hessian screen kindly hid the nether parts of the two officers but their heads and hats were in full view of us, the assembled group of officers. The red hat and the black side-cap appeared to be having a most animated conversation. We wondered who would move first and what the accepted protocol was for such a situation. As if in answer to our prayers, Mac, the 2/ic, rose and to a muffled cheer from the keen observers, gave a smart salute as he passed the genial General. What were you talking about, we asked, expecting to hear some secrets about the coming offensive. Bad stomachs, was the reply. Obvious really !

Later, restored to a more dignified position, our guest gave us a pep talk. It was terrible. That day I was to record that no commander should talk to his troops unless he can strike a cord and raise their enthusiasm. I fear that we officers parodied the Army Commander many times afterwards. When the Battalion was able to celebrate its annual Dashera festival, the 'joker party' put on a most amusing and accurate sketch of the General's visit, thunderbox, hessian screen and all. To this day I do not know how the men found out about the episode as only officers were near the scene of the retreat. Gurkha soldiers' comic turns are invariably topical, accurate, personal, but never cruel. I am sure that if the Army Commander had been a guest at the 1944 Dashera he would have laughed louder than most—without scurrying away to the nearest loo.

Although the Army Commander did not give any details he told us that the offensive which was to break through the Gothic Line was due to be launched in early September. This, he promised us, would be the beginning of the end ; Once the break through had been achieved then it would be an all-out attack and the Germans would not be given a chance to draw breath or make a stand or prepare any further defensive positions until they had been driven out of Italy. It all sounded too easy and I regret to say that there were many cynical comments after the General had departed. So many times had we seen and heard optimistic Intelligence officers forecasting that the German Army was in a bad way, with its morale low so that a large scale withdrawal was considered to be inevitable. And invariably in a matter of hours the Germans would give their answer in the shape of a fierce counter attack or bombard us with accurately directed mortar and artillery fire. Yes, we had heard it all before : we hoped the Army Commander was right but wondered. On the other hand there is no doubt that from Desmond down to the junior rifleman we were brim-ful of confidence in ourselves, even if our faith in those above was not very strong.

One point that the General had reiterated over and again was that once the pursuit had begun, the road discipline, convoy control and traffic arrangements had to be first class. He had mentioned that the Military Police would not be sufficient for this purpose and that each major unit would have to organise and train small teams to assist. His words were brought home to me next morning when the Adjutant told me that I was to be the unit traffic control officer. I remonstrated but to no effect, it was the Colonel's order. Anyway, I was informed, I would have a most interesting and hectic time once the break through had been achieved. I cannot remember my reply but I am sure it was a sarcastic one !

The Divisional plan for the move across to the Adriatic coast was shrouded in secrecy until the last moment. 5 and 7 Brigades went first while we in 11 Brigade remained behind near Trasimeno and tried to pretend that we were the whole Division. I do not know if such a deception plan fooled the German agents, it may have done for a time. Then on 23 August it was our turn to move. We were told that we would have to travel far and fast, Vienna via Venice was to be our destination !

The move across had been planned with meticulous care and was put into operation by efficient staff work. Each unit moved by night over roads that twisted and turned through hills and mountains. Vehicles were not allowed to use their head lights. No divisional signs were displayed at crossroads or direction arrows ; police and unit traffic posts were deployed to guide the vehicles along the appointed route. Before dawn broke the convoys had to be hidden among trees away from prying eyes ; only now do I appreciate how difficult it must have been for the staff planners and it is to their credit that the move of the whole division went smoothly and, as far as I know deceived the enemy agents during the early days as units advanced towards the Gothic Line outposts.

On 24 August the Battalion had assembled at Cantiana which was not far from the Adriatic coastline. Near Cantiano was a massive mountain, Point 1143, which, I was told, would be the objective for E. D. Smith and his six man traffic control team. While we were all laughing about it, the unfortunate Miles was told by Desmond that his D Company was to take the mountain. Miles thought the Colonel was joking but he was not. Guided by two Partisans and assisted by some mules, the unfortunate D Company struggled up to the summit of the impressive mountain only to find that it was theirs without a fight. What their feelings were I can only guess but it meant, for the remainder of the Battalion, that the chase was on : we went through the towns of Pianello, Gagli and then the most beautiful of them all, Urbino. We moved fast but the Germans moved faster. It was great stuff, it went to our heads and during the last three or four days of August we lived like victors and felt like conquerors as we liberated villages, to be greeted by cheering girls with bottles of wine and mouths generous with their kisses, inviting us to stay a while. Our Gurkhas had never seen white women behave in such a manner and, at first, were a trifle nonplussed. Their shyness did not last for long and they enjoyed the adulation and excitement as much as we did.

By 1 September we were a few miles south of the River Foglia. The Germans, we were told, had their main defences in the foot hills to the north of the valley. Ahead of us men from 5 Brigade were crossing the river and had begun probing the outer defences. For three days I had been busily engaged with traffic control duties which needed much patience, and kept us out of bed during most nights, as we tried to ensure the sleepy drivers of vehicles went in the correct and required direction.

11 Brigade followed the leading units of 5 Brigade at a discreet distance with its role being to exploit to the utmost any break through achieved by those in the van. At first all seemed to go well but when our fighter-bombers began dive bombing targets on the other side of the valley, we realised that the Germans had other ideas on how the battle for the Gothic Line was to be fought. No more villages were to be liberated without tough fighting first.

Desmond met all his British officers at an observation post, south of the River Foglia from where we could see the hills on the opposite side of the valley. It was not necessary for him to tell us that 5 Brigade was meeting with stiff opposition : all the signs and sounds of a struggle at close quarters were clearly evident. He explained that companies from the 9th Gurkha Rifles were now taking over the spearhead role and would be moving along the ridge from Monte Calvo towards the north, where another village, Tavoleto dominated the countryside around it.

Desmond repeated the optimistic forecast he had received from Brigade Headquarters earlier that day but without any conviction. He knew, as well as we did, that we would be in the fight, certainly within a day or two and, possibly, within hours. Meanwhile, there did not seem to be a role for me if operations reverted back to the slow-moving, relentless infantry fighting we had grown accustomed to elsewhere in Italy. Who would want traffic posts when we were fighting on our feet against a tough enemy in well prepared defences ? I was told to be patient. By a quirk of fate I did not have to wait long.

Charlie Company's Eric Holton had come to attend the order's group in a jeep. When the meeting was over he jumped in the vehicle, only to back it into a deep ditch when turning. The jeep was not damaged but Eric hurt his back—and had to be evacuated to hospital. As soon as I heard the news my heart jumped in anticipation, even, though I was sorry that, once again, Eric was not going to lead his men. I never doubted that the Colonel would select anyone else to take over Charlie Company and, to this end, I went to Battalion Headquarters to hear if my appointment had been ratified.

Desmond and the Adjutant were discussing that very subject : they looked up when I entered then carried on as if I was not there. Two or three names were discussed but mine was not one of them. A newly joined officer, junior to me in age and service, seemed to be about to be selected. I was so amazed that at first words would not come. When they did, there was considerable feeling behind them. I was the obvious replacement, Charlie Company knew me, we had done reasonably well together on Monte Grillo, and what was the point in choosing a newly arrived officer to command them when I was available ? Desmond was surprised into silence ; I had never said boo to anyone senior to myself before, let alone the CO.

Ah, he said, but you are our traffic control expert. And the General has given strict instructions that unit TC teams must be readily available when the ' break out' north of the Gothic Line, begins. I exploded although I cannot remember what I said, fortunately perhaps. Certainly I made the point that an intelligent NCO with a knowledge of English, could carry out the TC duties as well as I could. And as for the break out—did the Colonel really think that was going to come ?

Desmond interrupted me in some anger : '' Shut up ! for Christ's sake, shut up. No one has spoken to me like that since I became CO. You had better go to C Company before I clap you in irons''. And he added a few more choice phrases which sent me flying before he changed his mind. Even after I had disappeared, I was worried in case he changed his decision about the appointment. I never really knew how his mind worked, his smiles could dissolve into bursts of anger for seemingly trivial reasons.

At Charlie Company I was greeted with warmth by friends. Subedar Krishnabahadur Gurung was as outspoken in his welcome as he had been in his criticism of me during our approach march towards Monte Grillo. Just the Sahib we wanted, he said, adding to my embarrassed surprise that Holton Sahib would never lead men into action again. Why I asked ? His blunt reply was that the Sahib had lost his nerve.

Maybe, maybe not. Such things happened to the bravest, to the best : something snapped so that the individual's deposit of courage dried up, ceased to function. Some called it battle fatigue, others gave it names cruelly descriptive of those unfortunate men who could no longer withstand the strain and stresses of fighting.

As I did not agree with the Subedar's opinion of Eric, which he had given in front of a handful of junior ranks, my first task as the newly reappointed Company Commander was to take him to one side and tick him off. He apologised for making the remarks in the hearing of his juniors but reiterated that all the men would be delighted to see me back as their Company Commander. We left it like that. We had to because I was due to move with the other company commanders in the Colonel's orders group while the Company followed later. For this move the whole Battalion would be carried forward in jeeps and trailers which had appeared from nowhere, another piece of excellent staff magic. The administrative planners accomplished many things which we tended to take for granted at the time.

The four rifle company commanders climbed into the back of the CO's Daimler, an armoured half-track vehicle. Alan Howard drove with a rather noisy Desmond sitting beside him. After a few minutes I realised that the Colonel had been drinking heavily and I sat primly in disapproving silence thereafter. Apart from Moreton (OC A Company), who had obviously been imbibing with his Colonel, I knew that the others shared my misgivings about this not being the time and place to be hitting the bottle. Our fears were realised when the road began to descend to the Foglia River. Desmond told Alan to stop the vehicle, which he did, he then cocked the Browning machine guns, mounted on the vehicle, and pointed them at the slopes near Monte Calvo on the other side of the river.

" To hell with those bloody Tedeski (Germans). Let's pepper the bastards up .... ", and then followed a flow of rich invective.

Someone, not me, tried to restrain him, which brought forth a few more choice phrases. Fortunately, Moreton was sober enough, as well as being on the same alcoholic wavelength, to warn Desmond that he would be firing at the 9th Gurkhas. The angry Colonel ordered Alan to drive on with all of us feeling ashamed and, speaking for myself, worried by the incident. Moreton was right. The morning light showed that the 9th Gurkhas would have been in the line of Desmond's erratic firing had he pressed the trigger. And then, God knows that would have happened : it might have led to Desmond's Court Martial or to our vehicle being attacked by angry 9th Gurkhas. Once more I was convinced that drinking and fighting was as lethal a combination as drinking and driving.

Desmond left us, his orders group, on the northern bank of the Foglia while he went forward to meet the Commander of 5 Brigade. I have no doubt that he arrived in a sober state as his journey forward was on foot. Realising that it might be hours before we were summoned, we settled down to rest in a small copse just as dawn was breaking. An hour or two later we were woken by Alan to be told that our men would be arriving shortly—and would we guide them to areas where they would be under cover ? Tired and bleary eyed Gurkha soldiers did not need any persuading to get their heads down : one of the hallmarks of a fighting soldier is his ability to snatch rest at each and every opportunity. Gurkhas can sleep anywhere, in great discomfort, oblivious to noise and to danger, unless it is near at hand.

My memory tells me that it was nearly midday when the Battalion orders group was instructed to go forward, on foot, to meet Desmond somewhere along the road beween Monte Calvo and Tavoleto. Each of us was escorted and accompanied by his runner, in my case Rifleman Rambahadur. We were instructed to maintain a generous interval because Desmond did not want his rifle company commanders to be written off by a single shell or mortar before they could participate in the oncoming battle. The walk through the recently captured village of Monte Calvo along the open hot road was an unpleasant one. The sun beat down only to be reflected from the white dust. Sweat poured off us, soon to be caked under a film of congealed dust thrown up by the occasional tank that passed us or by a jeep carrying casualties back to the forward medical reception centre. All around us there was clear evidence of the recent fighting. Monte Calvo was in ruins with burnt out tanks, abandoned equipment, a few corpses surrounded by huge nauseating blue flies ; ahead of us there was the sound of heavy firing by British tanks, the rattle of machine guns and the occasional retaliatory mortar ' stonk ' from the Germans.

I cannot say how long it took us to reach the rendezvous. It seemed like hours and certainly it was late afternoon when we met Alan Howard, who was wisely sheltering in a conveniently close ditch because the stretch of road near him seemed to be a favourite target for enemy mortar crews. Alan pointed to a small farmhouse on the other side of the exposed part of the road :

'' The Colonel is waiting for you below the house. From there you will be able to see our objective, Tavoleto. You are to cross the open stretch one by one, taking your runners with you''.

We decided to go in order of precedence, Able Company (Moreton), Baker (Trevor), Charlie (myself), and Dog Company, (Tim), with the unfortunate Alan Howard bringing up the rear. If anyone was to say to me that familiarity with shot, bomb and shell breeds contempt, I would call him a liar or deem him to be a complete moron. At the height of a battle at close quarters fear may be diminished temporarily, but watching my friends in cold blood ducking and weaving their way across open ground, while bombs burst near them was truly unnerving. Especially when I realised that my turn was still to come. If the walk up had not dehydrated me, then I would have ' pissed' myself in blue funk.

In the end we crossed without anyone being hit although Tim Brown and his runner had to go to ground when four bombs landed within feet of them. To our surprise they rose and unhurt joined us, breathless and shaken.

A serious faced Desmond greeted us behind a bank near the farm. Before he even spoke it was obvious that a tough assignment faced us. The 9th Gurkhas had met with a rebuff when trying to advance towards Tavoleto. British tanks, too, had not been able to move any further forward. Now it was to be our turn ; the mission was to capture Tavoleto before first light next morning. Before Desmond gave out detailed orders, in turn each of us crawled up the bank to be shown the village which stood on a ridge about two miles away. Its church tower was silhouetted against the setting sun and in that light shone like a beacon. Keeping the right direction with such an objective looked simple but nevertheless I warned Rambahadur that he would have to act as guide because it might be dark before the rest of the company appeared.

Desmond began his orders with an apology, which was not the most effective way of inspiring us, his subordinates. He explained that there would be little or no time for our platoon commanders to view the ground before us, although they were moving ahead of the main body and might arrive before it was completely dark. Then ; the Battalion would capture Tavoleto by first light tomorrow morning. The aim, his mission, was crystal clear and indeed the plan we were to adopt seemed simple in the exposition : all too simple as we were to discover.

In retrospect it is obvious that the whole process of deployment and attack was so rushed that the company commanders did not have time to even consider the practicalities or query the distressing lack of detail in Desmond's orders, for what in reality was a very ambitious venture. The 9th Gurkhas had tried to approach Tavoleto by the most direct route, along the axis of the road which clung to the top of the ridge before it led straight into the village. The Germans knocked out the leading tanks and brought the infantry to a halt by fire from well concealed machine gun posts, supplementing it all with heavy artillery and mortar fire. The direct approach, therefore, had proved costly and had ended in failure.

Desmond had no other alternative but to adopt a longer approach on the left flank, one that went round the side of the hill with the road as our right hand boundary. Having viewed the country twice since the war under peacetime conditions, I am sure that he selected the best route. Everything else in his plan was wrong, but I must not pre-empt my story.

His plan was in two phases, first, to surround and cut off the village during the night, then to begin the second phase which was to clear Tavoleto, using tanks and infantry after first light. By such a plan he hoped to avoid fighting in a built-up area during darkness. Apart from the problem of control our tanks would not have been able to operate in the village at night, without adding to the confusion as well as being extremely vulnerable themselves to enemy close quarter weapons. In Desmond's plan, Able and Dog Companies were to carry out the equivalent of a giant left hook, aiming to seize ground to the north and rear of the village. Once in position, they would not only prevent the defenders from the village escaping but, of more importance, stop reinforcements coming forward to their aid. Baker Company was to seal off the only other road into the village connecting it with Auditore, a town to the west, known to be another German stronghold. Again, B Company's role was to be the dual one of stopping the enemy moving into or out of Tavoleto. Finally, Charlie Company would be in reserve with the task of moving across country before taking up a position about a thousand yards away from Tavoleto, on the south side.

Desmond did not specify which rifle company would clear Tavoleto next morning. He indicated that it might be Baker Company moving in from the west or Charlie Company from the south : he said there were far too many imponderables for him to make a final decision at that moment. For Phase I there was to be no pre-arranged artillery fire plan and targets could not be requested except in a dire emergency. The command radio was not to be used until Battalion Headquarters issued a code word over the net although all company sets were to remain open on listening watch during the advance. The essence of the plan was the silent approach without fire and fury. It was a gamble, an Irishman's gamble, putting complete trust in his Gurkhas' ability to move long distances at night and then to surprise the enemy at close quarters. After all, he said, it is not as long an approach as the one you chaps did at Monte Grillo nor is the country nearly so difficult.

True, but at Monte Grillo we had twenty-four hours for reconnaissances, briefings, and preparation—and even then Charlie Company, under myself, lost the way !

If you wonder how I am able to recall the details of the struggle for Tavoleto so clearly, the explanation is that I helped to write the official account of the attack after the war, I have returned to revisit the village twice in peace time, and indeed, nearly thirty years after the attack, conducted a short battlefield tour for forty men of the 7th Gurkha Rifles, many of them sons, nephews and relations of the men who fought at Tavoleto between the 1st and 3rd September, 1944. In addition, on more than one occasion, the battle has been used as a cloth model exercise for British and Gurkha officers of the Regiments. In truth, I have had to live and relive these events many times since the war.

As soon as Desmond's orders were over, our platoon commanders arrived. The sun was a faint red glow as one by one I showed my four Gurkha officers the church tower of Tavoleto, silhouetted against the dying sunset. Of the intervening country little could be seen as it was shrouded in shadow ; we noticed vineyards and one or two houses but not the objective we had to reach, a dried river bed which was invisible even in daylight. Fortunately Charlie Company did not have to move until 8.30 p.m. (2030 hours), half an hour after the other three rifle companies set off. After Desmond had moved to the farm to establish his headquarters, we asked Alan if there was any more information known about the German defences in Tavoleto or the extent of their outposts. Unfortunately, the plan for the attack had been so hurried that our Intelligence officer had not been able to liaise with his opposite number in the other Gurkha battalion so, in effect, nothing was known about the enemy except that he had the road on our right axis well and truly covered.

The Colonel's plan to surround and seal off Tavoleto was too ambitious, far too hurried and most indifferently planned. Far too much was left to chance but unbeknown to us, his subordinates, the pressure had come from the very top. Progress on the coastal plain near the Adriatic was satisfactory but inland, especially around Tavoleto, the Germans were holding firm—and were using the high ground to advantage with their observers directing artillery and mortar fire onto the flanks of the advancing British Army. ''Tavoleto has to be taken and taken now''; this order was passed down from headquarter to headquarters while the 7th Gurkhas had been moving forward during the late afternoon. Such a chain reaction caught Desmond off balance : he received a firm order and this plan was the result. After the battle for Tavoleto was over, I had time to think and wonder what Colonel Gerry Gordon's reaction would have been to such steam rolling from above !

At the time on 1 September, I had no real misgivings, possibly because Charlie Company had been given a minor role as reserve company during the difficult first phase. With the other companies advancing thirty minutes before us, virtually over the same ground for the first mile, the Gurkha officers and I did not anticipate that we would meet any Germans and certainly not before first light next morning. We were grateful for the extra half an hour's delay as a sort of meal was eaten, in contrast to the leading companies who went off into battle on empty stomachs. I saw them leave at eight o'clock and with some time to wait, went to see Desmond in his temporary quarters in the deserted farmhouse. I found him tense and nervy, trying to hide his anxiety behind a boisterous cheerfulness. This was not in his character but was an indication that he had been rushed into something about which he probably had considerable doubts and misgivings. He produced a large tot of gin for me which I accepted with reluctance but behind his back added an even larger quantity of water to it. The Colonel's easy smile and smooth Irish blarney put me at ease although I wondered whether my commanding officer had not asked too much from his battalion. It was too late now ; the gin had begun to dispel some of my fears. Who knows, perhaps Gerry had pulled back reacting to the British thrust along the coast ? In that case it might be a quiet evening walk without any shooting. It was time to go.

'' Good luck, Birdie,'' said the Colonel, and to my surprise he held out his hand.

Perhaps after all Desmond did anticipate that Charlie Company would be doing some fighting within the next few hours ?

Rambahadur was waiting outside, together we climbed over a bank and joined the Company. Subedar Krishnabahadur reported that all were present and ready to go. I was just about to give the order to move when loud sounds of battle dispelled any illusion that the Germans had decided to evacuate the village. The ' burp, burp' of spandau machine guns and the dull thud of grenades, mingled and combined with shouts of excited and frightened men, indicated that at least one of our companies had met the enemy. I waited by the radio but no message came while Battalion headquarters maintained complete silence. This meant that we had to carry on as planned and we set off towards our objective, over a mile away.

Ahead of us hayricks were burning, ignited, probably deliberately, by German tracer bullets ; occasionally we could see a hazy figure illuminated by the fire but it was impossible to say who was friend and who was foe. Behind me the company signaller moved with his headphones on but, as yet, no one had broken wireless silence.

Sherbahadur Sunwar's platoon was in the lead at the head of a long line because I had decided that it was the most effective way of keeping control especially as the companies ahead would have cleared the area through which we were passing—in theory anyway. Although I had learnt my lesson at Monte Grillo, not to act as leading scout, it soon became apparent that Rambahadur and I would have to be near the front section because no one else had had a chance to see the ground in daylight. Occasionally when the ground dipped or where the hedges were unduly thick, it was not possible to see our guiding star, the church tower of Tavoleto. Nevertheless, direction finding was not difficult although by now we were all mystified by the sound of fighting on our left flank.

On we went without any idea as to where the other companies were or how they were faring. The Battalion wireless net maintained a strict silence which I found perplexing as at least one of the companies had met heavy resistance. When we descended into a small ravine, I estimated that if my calculations were correct, then we had reached our objective— and at the bottom there was a dried up river bed which confirmed my suspicions. So, as far as Charlie Company was concerned, Phase I had gone according to plan.

The ground rose on our right up to the crest of the ridge, along which ran the main road : it seemed probable that in daylight we might be overlooked so that a platoon might have to guard that flank. Leaving Subedar Krishnabahadur Gurung to allocate temporary positions in the ravine to the three platoons, I set off up a path which climbed towards the road ; with me went Rambahadur and another rifleman as escorts. Rounding a bend we saw the faint outline of a house nearby. Motioning the two riflemen to follow I started to crawl up the bank so as to obtain a closer look at the house. At the top I slowly raised my head. The building was about twenty-five to thirty yards away and appeared to be a medium sized farmhouse. As I watched, the front door opened and out came four enemy who were speaking rather heatedly in German as if arguing among themselves. One carried a machine gun. For a few seconds I gazed but did nothing. I sensed that Rambahadur had slithered his way up by my side, then heard a soft gasp of surprise before I saw that he was bringing his rifle up into a firing position. I put a restraining hand on his arm, while we watched and listened. Then, for no apparent reason, one of the Germans shouted something and in a flash they dashed behind the house to disappear.

My mind was full of questions then which remain unanswered today, over thirty years later. Why didn't I fire or let Rambahadur fire ? Those Germans were sitting ducks at that range : there was little risk involved and it was most unlikely that there were any of their friends nearby. What were they doing ? Were they a machine gun detachment whose task had been to harass us at a distance, delaying our deployment and advance ? Had they seen or heard us, was that the reason for their sudden flight ? To Rambahadur, who asked me in some fury why I had allowed the ' dushman' to escape, my reply was that I did not want to reveal Charlie Company's presence in that forward area until I had to. On the face of it, sound tactics. Now I suspect that I did the right thing but for the wrong reason. To kill in hot blood, in a crisis and in an emergency, is something which, as a professional soldier, I recognise as inevitable, my duty. When I have had to do this, no sense of guilt has remained to haunt me afterwards. But to shoot down four men who were so near and so defenceless, seemed different, akin to the cold blooded murder committed by gunmen in many parts of today's unhappy world. That is but one side of the case, however ; inadvertently, or even advertently, I may have been responsible for inflicting casualties on my own side. That machine gun crew was allowed to escape and its members may have killed and maimed men of Charlie Company at a later stage in the battle for Tavoleto. Fortunately, I will never know if they did do so but happily too, I have never worried about my decision to allow those four Germans to live.

Leaving the two riflemen to act as sentries on our open flank I returned to the Company and sent for the Gurkha officers. The Subedar told me where he had positioned the platoons : in return I explained that a platoon would have to move up towards the road to cover us on that side. Selecting 9 Platoon for this task, I returned with Jemedar Jitbahadur and showed him what he had to defend although I decided to leave the farmhouse empty—in daylight it would have been an obvious target in full view of any observers in Tavoleto village.

Having finalised our disposition, I gave the order to dig : the men began digging as quietly as they could behind the banks and any other available cover. In the darkness it was not easy and as dawn approached, we had to make various adjustments to the tentative positions selected during the night. While I was visiting 9 Platoon, three Germans walked down from the main road and without a shot being fired or even a challenge, the Gurkhas seized them from behind, and made them prisoner. Back at Company Headquarters, I found that they were badly frightened, visibly scared of the Gurkhas holding their much publicised kukris. One prisoner, an Austrian, spoke excellent English. He explained how glad they were to see me, a fellow European, because they had heard fearsome stories about the legendary Gurkhas. Many were, of course untrue, highly coloured by the German propaganda experts. The Austrian pleaded with me not to leave them alone with the Gurkhas. I reassured him that they would come to no harm ; as if to prove my words, within minutes Rambahadur and his friends were offering our captives cigarettes and scraps of food they could ill afford to give away. This was not the first occasion that I was to be annoyed at over-fraternisation by our men with German prisoners. I am sorry if this does not sound like the blood thirsty Gurkhas, heroes of many past battles, but in reality the Nepalese are a gentle, easy going and kindly people. When they are roused, however, for good reason or for foul, then they can be transformed into angry furies ; on such occasions a firm restraining hand is a necessity and not always easy to apply.

The Austrian prisoner was a well educated man who had spent more than two years in England before the war. He and his companions were glad to be prisoners ; they realised that the war was all but lost and they wished to survive to see the peace rather than die in battle for a cause in which they had no faith or trust. Why had they moved down the path, I asked : the reply was that they had been on patrol without any prior knowledge that a company of Gurkhas was hiding in the ravine area. At such a time I could not spare escorts to take the prisoners back to headquarters nor had communications been established. After consulting his friends, the Austrian gave his word of honour that they would not try and escape. Subedar Krishnabahadur and I agreed to let them sit in the middle of company headquarters under Rambahadur's watchful eye. Within minutes they were all engaged in an animated conversation using a mixture of broken Italian and a few words of English ; it was evident that our captives had no desire to run away to fight another day.

Not long before dawn Battalion Headquarters began contacting the companies on the radio, breaking the wireless silence which they had imposed, and possibly maintained throughout the night. I have never been able to find out whether the complete embargo was deliberate or accidentally prolonged by our radio not functioning at certain times. No matter except that 2 September saw the Battalion in some disarray ; it was to take at least an hour before Colonel Desmond heard how his rifle companies had fared during the night

While it was important that I also learnt where Able, Baker and Dog Companies were, the early morning light did not give me a chance to stay by the company headquarters radio because the site we had selected in the dark proved to be in full view of an unfriendly machine gun, which sent us scurrying for cover. No one was hit but it meant that the Germans in and around the village now knew that there was a force of Gurkhas hiding in the river bed, far too near to them for comfort and, unfortunately for us, at a convenient distance to be shot at by their dreaded mortars. Such a thought spurred us all into further digging ; rightly or wrongly I abandoned a tactical defensive layout and closed the company into a tight ring, using the rear slopes to the maximum advantage for protection against the mortar bombs that would soon be searching us out in the ravine.

Although such a decision undoubtedly saved many lives, I was probably unwise to discount the possibility of a full scale counter attack which, if it had been launched, would have been on top of us before we had even appreciated the danger. I was to realise how lucky I was that day because, later, the Germans swept down against D Company which held firm but from properly organised defences. I fear that Charlie Company would have been engulfed in similar circumstances.

While we were still sorting ourselves out, burrowing into the soft ground like frightened moles, my signaller had been recording the encoded map references of the other companies as these were being relayed back to Battalion Headquarters. After deciphering and plotting them on a map, our first message to my superiors was to ask them to repeat corrected versions. Confirmation came but no corrections. I was astounded and not at all cheered by the news. The Colonel's plan had gone sadly awry ; instead of Charlie Company being in reserve in a lay back position, we were closest to Tavoleto in a most dangerous position and the enemy knew where we were. On our left flank A and D companies were at least a thousand yards to the west, across a valley on another ridge, while B company, although nearby, was slightly to the rear, again on our left flank.

I am not able to tell the stories of the other companies because I do not know any details. They veered to the left, to the west, after stumbling into German machine gun detachments, hidden in the orchards and vineyards. They tried to find a way round but could not do so, which was not surprising because you will recall that the commanders had seen little of the ground during daylight and, moreover, nothing had been known about the enemy's dispositions except on the right flank. What the other companies did do was to clear a path for us so that Charlie Company was able to walk unopposed to the ravine and its dried up, stony riverbed.

It was a real muddle for Desmond to sort out especially as he had Brigade Headquarters and above, pressing him hard, ordering him to capture Tavoleto as soon as possible. His problems were not made any easier by the fact that the slopes forward of his headquarters in the farmhouse were in full view of observers in the village. The Colonel might have been able to come forward on his own but without staff officers and signallers to run Tactical headquarters, without radios to communicate with the companies, with the guns, and with Brigade Headquarters, such a move would have been pointless. He could not move his headquarters forward until the evening. Without being able to consult his company commanders, or learn their views, and glean local intelligence, Colonel Desmond was in an unenviable position. For security reasons radio conversations could but give an incomplete picture which often led to misunderstandings and misconceptions. Rightly he put his faith in establishing a field telephone link with the forward companies. In fact, line-laying signallers had moved behind each company during the night but in the confusion these men had gone astray. Thereafter gallant efforts were made to run cables out to the rifle companies and the signal platoon lost several casualties while trying to do so. Only the courage of these line parties enabled battalion headquarters to speak to us by telephone before midday. Even then our line was cut by enemy mortar fire about two hours later and I never spoke on the telephone again before we began our assault on Tavoleto.

After we had the benefit of communication by a relatively secure field telephone, Alan Howard told me that the Germans had pulled back from Tavoleto or, at least that was the message Intelligence in higher headquarters had relayed down to the 7th Gurkhas. Disregarding my rude reply, he went on to say that a patrol was to be sent from our location into the village at once. Apart from being angry I was horrified at the suggestion but was firmly ordered to get on with it and stop belly-aching. I was tempted to go myself, but Subedar Krishnabahadur made it quite clear that he would report such an action to the ''10 Sahib''.

Naik Chaturdhoj Limbu was the unfortunate NCO to whom I gave instructions for the most hazardous of patrols. Subedar Krishnabahadur Gurung's advice was that Chaturdhoj would be the best choice for something that required more than blind, devoted obedience by the patrol commander. The slimly built Chaturdhoj stood before me ; he had a soft voice and a shy smile, a man who moved with the natural grace of an athlete. He listened in silence to the orders, then asked a couple of intelligent questions before returning to select two companions from his section. Even if I failed to conceal my indignation at the task he was being given, Chaturdhoj accepted it as just another duty, something he expected as a soldier on active service.

After they had spotted Chaturdhoj's patrol moving towards the village in broad daylight, the German defenders had three choices open to them. They could open fire to stop them covering more than a few yards from our ravine which, of course, would have been an easy end to Chaturdhoj's mission, provided that he and his men were not hit. This is what I hoped would happen. Or the enemy could hold their fire drawing the three Gurkhas into a position where they could eliminate them in an ambush. Or they could let the patrol enter the village only to capture the men as prisoners. Intertwined with these possibilities was our desire to find out more about any German outposts which we suspected lay between us and Tavoleto itself. Although I did not want to risk the patrol, I hoped that some benefits might result out of the ill conceived venture. It was this last point that influenced us into selecting the best junior NCO in the company to lead the patrol.

Ten minutes later the three young Gurkhas reported to Company Headquarters before setting off. They had stripped off all equipment and carried Tommy guns only, wearing canvas PT shoes instead of the normal service boots. Their impassive faces displayed no emotion when we wished them luck. Before they crawled over the top of the bank, the Subedar and I went to an observation post, relieving the two riflemen on duty there. We lay with our binoculars, ready to wait and watch.

Thanks to Chaturdhoj, not one of the three possibilities mentioned in the earlier paragraph came to pass. His first problem was to cover some fifty yards of open country before they reached the cover of a large vineyard. From our vantage point we were unable to see them but visualized the men as they crawled across on a very hot day, well aware that they were in a most conspicuous position. A few minutes elapsed, then a German spandau opened up from a small outhouse below the main road, firing tracer bullets at the field in front of us. As the gun fired a few bursts Krishnabahadur took a compass bearing so that we could record its exact location for future reference. After it stopped firing, all was silence once more. In trepidation we waited but no one returned. I was sick with rage and deeply ashamed that I had agreed to send the three men out to certain death.

Leaving Subedar Krishnabahadur, I ran back to Company Headquarters and asked to speak to the Commanding Officer on the telephone. Fortunately, perhaps, he was not available so that Alan Howard received my angry bitter comments which I asked to be relayed back to 'the top brass', to the officers who claimed that the Germans had withdrawn ; let them do their own dirty work in future.

Poor Alan : fortunately he had a calm unflappable nature and was used to histrionics from temperamental company commanders.

Back at the observation post I found an excited Krishnabahadur. He claimed that he had caught a glimpse of our men well beyond the vineyards, moving up towards the village. It seemed most improbable, and as we did not see anything for many more minutes, I found it increasingly difficult to believe his story. But it was true, and somehow those gallant soldiers arrived back with us although, once again, they had to run the gauntlet across the final stretch, over the open field. Chaturdhoj brought back much invaluable information ; they had seen and avoided several German outposts which they were able to plot with accuracy on our map.

"And why" I said, " Did you disobey my orders, Chature ? Did I not tell you to come back as soon as you were spotted ?"

He grinned, realising that I was praising him for the results of the reconnaissance, admiring him for cold-blooded courage and thanking God for his safe return. After the men had rejoined their platoon I sat down and scribbled a citation for Chaturdhoj Limbu, recommending that he should be awarded an IDSM (Indian Distinguished Service Medal), and the two riflemen, MM's (Military Medals), or at the worst, Mention in Despatches. Over the field telephone I repeated these words of praise while relaying the information brought back by the patrol. I promised to send the citations back with the next person due to return to Battalion Headquarters.

A few minutes later, possibly around three o'clock in the afternoon, Alan phoned to say that important orders were being sent forward by hand of a Signal's NCO. He was about to give me the gist of the orders in general terms when a heavy bombardment began, directed at the farmhouse, our Battalion headquarters. Obviously the NCO or messengers had been seen by the Germans. The field cable was cut, never to be repaired before we left our position in the ravine at midnight. This was a bitter blow because although radio communications were working, the Germans had introduced a Hindustani speaker into our Battalion Command net : on occasions this gentleman joined in our conversations and made it clear to us that even messages in Nepali (Gurkhali) could be understood by the enemy. All we could do was wait for the messenger who was bringing forward the awaited written orders.

When the NCO arrived, I wished that the bombardment had sent him back to Battalion Headquarters. The orders he brought were akin to those we had received in Cassino when some joker gave us the Monastery as a target to attack in daylight. Now I read that Charlie Company was to attack and capture Tavoleto, beginning the assault at midnight. At first I could not believe my eyes and it took me a little time to realise that other sub units were involved, that it was more than just a solo attack by our ninety strong company.

The orders were written by Alan on an ordinary message pad ; that, at least, meant that they were concise and simple, unlike the lengthy detailed efforts produced by budding commanders at the Army Staff College. 2/7 GR was to attack and capture Tavoleto by 0600 hours 3 September. Phase I was to see Able Company on the left seizing the Tavoleto-Auditore Road, on the west side of the village. At the same time a company of the Cameron Highlanders was to make a limited advance on the east side of the road above us in order to divert the attention of the Germans from Phase II, the piece de resistance, produced by Charlie Company at midnight precisely.

During Phase I and at the beginning of our advance, the Corps artillery was to batter away at the village on a timed programme. Indeed, the only detailed part of the orders was the fire plan and that appeared to be inflexible. For some reason or other, the one FOO (Forward Observation Officer), allotted to the Battalion, was left with the static D Company instead of moving forward with Able or Charlie Companies where he would have been invaluable, switching the fire of the guns to help us advance if pinned down. Tactical headquarters (Battalion) was scheduled to move forward after completion of Phase I and, if necessary, the CO would use Baker Company, supported by tanks, to clear up any pockets of resistance that remained in the village after daylight next day.

I find it impossible now to describe what my feelings were like as I studied that insignificant piece of paper in a foxhole on 2 September 1944. While the Gurkha officers and I had anticipated that Charlie Company would have to play a major part in the capture of Tavoleto, we had imagined that the attack would be made in daylight, involving at least two companies in conjunction with tanks, clearing the village in as orderly a manner as possible. Attacking a large village at night promised to be a deadly confused muddle, a task beyond the capacity of a single rifle company. I was worried by the lack of information known about our immediate enemy ; Chaturdhoj's patrol had revealed where some of his outposts were but we had no idea of what lay beyond them. An air photograph had been attached to the orders but it was hazy and of little value. Unfortunately for us it did not reveal a high wall around the centre of the village which enclosed the Church and some other buildings. That wall was to stop us dead in our tracks and so nearly cause disaster.

While my confused brain tried to make some sort of plan, Subedar Krishnabahadur Gurung had collected the three platoon commanders near the spot from where we could see the Church tower and some of the village on the sky line. When they saw my face they realised that Charlie Company faced a tough, dangerous battle. When I finished their faces showed disbelief and incredulity. Their first questions were not about tactics or anything in my detailed orders : rather did they ask how one company on its own could possibly clear such a village by night, had I queried the orders with the Commanding Sahib, how could any of us survive ? It was virtually impossible for a youngster of twenty-one to reassure older and far more experienced men that the plan would work, and could and must succeed. In my heart I agreed with everything the Gurkha officers said but when Jemedar Abidal continued to moan, repeating over and over again, '' Morio, morio, hami sabai morchhan'' (Dead, dead, we will all die), a deep despair caused me to explode in anger, telling him to shut up. A chastened group of officers then considered my orders, to ask a few questions before returning to brief their platoons.

My plan was as basic as the one produced by the Colonel. At zero hour, midnight, we were to advance with two platoons leading, 7 on the left and 9 on the right, with company headquarters and 8 Platoon moving between them, a few yards to the rear. I laid down a rate of advance to conform with the timed artillery programme. After we reached the village, the Church tower was to be the dividing line between the assaulting platoons : I was not to know that the wall below the Church would make such a boundary impossible. According-ing to the air photo there was a street on either side of the Church so that the leading platoons were instructed to clear these as best they could. I realised that there would be a possibility of some determined Germans remaining to fight it out : if these could not be eliminated during the night then the platoon commanders were to leave them, press on and move out of the village to the north. On the air photo-graph we selected a tentative company position which, I hoped, would stop any enemy reinforcements entering the village and after daylight came, enable Baker Company to mop up anyone who was still resisting in the village. There was probably more to my orders than the above bare outlines but basically that was how we proposed to capture Tavoleto.

After the orders group had finished, I deliberately followed Jemedar Abidal Limbu to sit nearby while he briefed 7 Platoon about the battle. Although he conveyed little optimism or spirit, he refrained from telling his men that the mission ahead promised death rather than victory.

A radio message awaited me at Company Headquarters which stated that food would be brought forward after dark by men from the Battalion defence platoon, acting as porters. Another coded item revealed that ' They' (Intelligence) were still optimistically fore-casting a German withdrawal along our sector ; Alan had added a note to say that the assessment was not confirmed ! By now we were extremely hungry as over twenty-four hours had elapsed since we had last fed. Tea and biscuits in the morning had helped to stave off the pangs of hunger a little but we looked forward to the arrival of the porters with anticipation.

At dusk we stood to. Apart from one or two sniper shots, the enemy had left us alone in the late afternoon. It did not take me long to go round our small tight perimeter nor was I in the mood for cheerful repartee with men who were hungry as well as being apprehensive at what the night would bring. After fifteen minutes of relative inactivity, I told the Company to stand down reverting to our normal sentries. With about three hours to midnight, zero hour, there appeared to be a chance to rest but a few minutes later the Germans dictated otherwise.

From west of the village a determined group of enemy swept down the ridge, on our left, and attacked D Company. Although we were out of the line of fire and across the valley, the fierce fight sounded as if it was but a few yards away. The firing, the shouts, the screams, meant that the attack had been pressed home to close quarters but as far as I could judge from garbled confused messages on the radio, Dog Company was holding firm—albeit with difficulty. It had been impossible to ascertain whether the Germans intended anything more than a delaying attack, to throw us off balance : my theory is and was that they expected the Battalion's assault to be launched up the ridge on the west, which explained their attack against D Company.

This unexpected demonstration of German power had a most demoralising effect on Charlie Company's morale. Nearby, I could hear Subedar Krishnabahadur and the Company Havildar-Major assessing our chances of capturing the village as nil. In the afternoon our assignment had seemed possible only if the enemy had been contemplating a withdrawal from the Tavoleto area. Now all was changed : not only were the Germans standing firm but the latest moves showed that they had reserves to spare, and more. It did not need the remarks of my subordinates to convince me that it was sheer madness for us to be hurled against the village at midnight. My fear was more than just a personal one ; I was frightened, yes, but the thought that some ninety Gurkhas under my command might be wiped out before dawn next morning was a daunting, horrifying thought. But what could I do ? The field telephone cable had been cut, Dog Company's battle was naturally taking priority on the Battalion radio net with an endless stream of operational messages and requests for artillery support, I felt powerless with my spirits at a lowest ebb ever. In desperation I decided to walk across to Baker Company in the hopes that their field telephone link with the Colonel had not been broken ; I could then discuss our impending attack in an open, secure fashion with Desmond, in the hope of persuading him to cancel or postpone our attack at midnight.

A rather unwilling Rifleman Rambahadur led the way to Baker Company. Apart from his error in Cassino, Rambahadur was a most reliable guide, with an excellent sense of direction at night. His reluctance had been caused by a genuine fear that with the fighting so near Baker Company, we would find their men trigger-happy and might be shot when approaching their position. Fortunately, our fears were not realised, the sentry who challenged us led the way to Trevor's Company Headquarters.

I cannot remember a bigger and deeper dugout than the one from which Trevor emerged. How the hell it had been constructed in the few hours we had been hiding below Tavoleto I cannot imagine. Trevor had film star looks, a big handsome man who was an experienced but cautious company commander. He poked his head out but did not come out into the open. I told him that our attack was crazy, I wanted to use his telephone and I intended telling Desmond that I refused to lead Charlie Company to certain death. Trevor tried calming me down. He said, quite categorically, that I would be risking court martial if I spoke in such terms to the Colonel. Moreover, he added, it was not just a case of Charlie Company attacking Tavoleto on its own ; a detailed fire plan had been produced and was due to start shortly, the Cameron Highlanders were about to make a diversionary raid against the high ground on the east end of the road, and our own A Company was poised to begin its part in the attack.

'' You will have to go in, Birdie, and the sooner you get back to your Company the better''. And having said that, Trevor disappeared into his dugout like a gigantic mole.

Realising that I could do no more, I indicated to Rambahadur that we would return to our Company. My companion had listened to the exchange of words between Trevor and myself although I imagined that with his lack of English, Rambahadur would have understood but little. Not so. What Rambahadur lacked in classroom education was more than made up by natural commonsense which he displayed when saying quietly to me :

'' Baker Company Sahib is dead scared. How many men did it take to construct that huge dugout ? Of course he did not want you to speak to the Commanding Sahib : if Charlie Company does not go in, then Baker Company would be selected by Colonel Sahib instead. Better we do the dirty work ourselves, Sahib''.

Rambahadur, my Rambahadur, a man of seventeen or eighteen years, did more to change my despairing fear into an obstinate grim determination. Charlie Company would attack Tavoleto whatever the cost and however ill-conceived the plan might be.

The Allied fire plan was due to begin at eleven p.m. (2300 hours), which would cover the Camerons on our right, and Able Company on our left, as they began moving towards their objectives. We arrived back at our Company Headquarters a few minutes before the bombardment began to tell the dejected Subedar Krishnabahadur Gurung that there was to be no postponement. Then, a few miles to the south, the Corps artillery opened up, and the night was full of noise and thunder once more. Although we were lurking in low ground, the constant whining of shells above our heads seemed alarmingly close. The already battered village of Tavoleto was caught in a maelstrom of hate and fury, the explosives smashed and pounded the shell of a village to ruins. Realising that there might be some form of retaliation, particularly as the Germans knew where all our companies were, those men not on sentry duty were told to remain under ground, protected by their foxholes and weapon pits. After Able Company had begun its advance we waited anxiously for news on how it was progressing but no messages were heard before midnight.

The Germans, having disrupted D Company on our left, now decided to strike at us. Two ranging mortar bombs landed in the ravine and then a few seconds later, came a vicious tornado of bombs bang on target, searching out our position with uncanny thoroughness. In Cassino we had been at the receiving end of many stonks but this one at Tavoleto was far more frightening. It was pin point shooting expertly controlled by an observer who must have known exactly where we were hiding. The noise was accentuated by the narrow ravine ; there was nothing we could do except cower in our fox holes praying that our earlier digging would safeguard us against everything except a direct hit. The onslaught lasted for five minutes at the most, the noise was unceasing so that it was impossible to know who had been hit and who had survived because no man, however brave, would have dared to have emerged from cover unless the bombardment had temporarily deranged him. Bombs continued to crash towards us until one hit the other end of the Headquarters dugout. There was a flash, a crash, the Subedar was flung sideways winding me with his elbow. I heard a scream and shouting because the bombardment had stopped. The last bomb had smashed our dugout.

Willing hands helped to pull us out. By a miracle, only two riflemen had been hit—and one of them was the company signaller. He appeared to have been badly wounded in the stomach although his first question was to ask for his radio set. Rambahadur found it smashed in pieces but I reassured the wounded Gurkha that it was serviceable and someone else would operate it. Now there was no means of communication with anyone ; we would not hear how the diversionary attacks were progressing, it was impossible to ask for guns to support us at any stage in the attack, no longer could Desmond let us know about any change of plan nor could I relay back details of the punishment handed out by the German mortars.

I looked at my watch, there were twenty minutes to go before the attack was due to begin. The Subedar Sahib went from platoon to platoon to check on casualties and arrange for their evacuation. We were astounded when the total losses proved to be but one rifleman killed and four wounded. The wounded posed a problem because we had no means of asking Battalion Headquarters to send forward stretcher bearers to collect them nor could I spare the equivalent of a section to carry the men back to the RAP. Fortunately the cool head of Subedar Krishnabahadur Gurung produced a solution : he would go to B Company and ask Trevor for a carrying party. Having despatched the wounded, Krishnabahadur would try to rejoin us somewhere in Tavoleto, or failing that, at our Phase II location which we hoped to have seized before morning light came next day.

Deep concern for the wounded had taken my mind off the most vital part of the night's drama, our attack at 0001 hours. Rambahadur went to call the three platoon commanders and a minute later they stood before me. Let us synchronise watches, I said, it is now ten minutes to twelve. In five minutes time lead your platoons up the bank, 7 on the left and 9 on the right, 8 Platoon to concentrate here where we are standing. The Gurkha officers had no spark of enthusiasm whatever. Jemedar Abidal murmured something about '' I don't think the lads will get out of their foxholes''.

His words stirred my anger as if he had poured iodine into an open wound : in fury I shouted that it was his job to get them out even if he had to use his tommy gun to do so. Above us two figures appeared out of the night, a young British officer and a sergeant from the Cameron Highlanders. The officer shouted :

'' Is that 5 platoon, what the hell are you doing down there ?''

'' We're not your bloody 5 platoon—we are the 2/7 Gurkhas and you're on the wrong side of the road''. In despair the young man asked if we had seen his men. '' No'', I said, '' and I'm trying to get my Gurkhas ready for an attack''. They disappeared into the night. To this day I do not know if they found the missing platoon. That young man had a problem but in a minute or two, I had a bigger one on my hands. Five minutes to zero hour and the leading platoons were not even near the start line.

In fury I went first to 7 Platoon and then to 9, cursing the Gurkha officers and their NCOs for not getting a grip of the men. My anger was for everybody, the Germans, the Gurkha officers, the Colonel, the top brass for telling us that the enemy was withdrawing and not least for myself. Murder was in my heart and the intensity of my feelings stirred subordinate commanders into immediate action. They began grabbing men, manhandling them out of foxholes, cuffing, belabouring them with curses until in a short time, the two assaulting platoons reported that they were ready to go. I went to the front, consulted my watch and then shouted :

" Come on, Charlie Company, we can take Tavoleto and we will do so. Let us pay the Germans back for all the ' dukha' (punishment) we've just had. Move ; 7 and 9, move now".

For a second no one moved, then 9 Platoon under Jemedar Jitbahadur went forward a few yards, very slowly. God, I thought, we really have had it, no food, no guts left and a suicidal attack. In desperation I shouted :

" What about your proverb—it's better to die than be a coward ? Right, stay here ; Rambahadur and I will go forward alone. Ramu, come on".

The effect was electrifying, as if I had touched open nerves to un-leash all the pent up fear, frustration, anger, all compounded by hunger and lack of sleep. On our left Jemedar Jitbahadur shrieked "Ayo Gurkhali", the cry was repeated on the right by 7 Platoon—then they were off. At last, they were moving but not as I intended, not according to the orders that had been explained to them during the afternoon. A steady advance should have been maintained for the first two or three hundred yards, before we met the first German machine gun post. All my orders and instructions were forgotten ; the leading platoons set off like a pack of hounds baying for blood, shouting and shrieking as if they were charging against the final objective. With the other battlefield noises continuing as before, there was no chance of my voice being heard—anyway they had already crossed the first field and nothing, short of death, was going to stop them. In truth I had unleashed the hounds of war.

Our Regimental History recorded a comment by a Camerons officer :

" What's going on in Tavoleto is nobody's business".

After the battle was over, friends were to confirm that the noise was unearthly, one that could be heard miles away. What it sounded like to the German defenders I cannot imagine. It was to be the first but by no means the last time that I was to thank the Almighty for putting me on the same side as the Gurkhas. On the night of 2/3 September 1944 they struck terror into my heart only because I had lost control of the two assaulting platoons within minutes of the advance beginning.

Jemedar Sherbahadur Sunwar, OC 8 Platoon, walked immediately behind me as we followed after the missing platoons. I did not want to lose control of the reserve platoon. At a brisk pace we made for the Church tower of Tavoleto, from where came a hell of a row as Gurkhas and Germans clashed with grenades and machine guns, their shouts and shrieks combining to heighten the confusion. We went forward non-tactically, in a single file, on the assumption that the enemy would have fled before the leading platoons. No doubt the majority had done so but, possibly in fear, one or two went to ground, only to bob up as we came out of the night.

When I was leading the column near a small farmhouse I saw a flash out of the corner of my eye ; then a giant wearing heavy tipped boots hacked my left foot from under me, down I crashed to the ground. It was all so sudden that it took me a couple of seconds to realise that the giant was a bullet fired from the top room of the house. At first there was no pain, just complete surprise, followed by shock. I lay as if dead, realising that I was an easy target to the enemy sniper should he see that I was still alive. Rambahadur, who had been walking a few feet behind, had taken cover somewhere : he shouted out in Gurkhali warning me not to move while they went behind the house to attack the sniper. The German was foolish to lean out and begin firing at the sound of the Gurkha's voice. Obviously he assumed that I was dead. It was my chance, I gripped the butt of my tommy gun, put my finger on the trigger and let rip. His body fell from the window riddled by bullets. There was no joy in my heart— only relief that I was still alive.

Sherbahadur and Rambahadur dashed forward and knelt beside me. The shock was wearing off. Rambahadur cut the bottom of my trouser leg away and tried to look at the wound. I put my hand down and in panic felt it was wet with blood. '' Bind it up quickly Ramu. Remember Keightly Sahib. Put a field dressing on as tightly as you can''.

Gradually the sense of panic disappeared when I realised that the wound was not a serious one. No bone had been broken, the bullet had gone through the lower half of my left foot without apparently causing any permanent damage—I hoped. Gently but firmly Rambahadur tended my wound. For some minutes we had forgotten about Tavoleto and our friends who had gone ahead. Belatedly I remembered. I ordered Jemedar Sherbahadur to take his platoon forward to the Church tower, his appointed objective in the first phase of the attack.

'' Right, Sahib. You must go back to the RAP. Rambahadur and the company runner will carry you back''.

'' No, Jemedar Sahib, this is only a flesh wound. The two lads can help me forward and I will meet you below the Church tower. 8 Platoon's help may be needed so go quickly. Until I arrive you must command the company. Off you go, Sahib''.

Believe me it was not a heroic gesture that made me decide to go forward rather than return as a walking casualty to the RAP. It would have taken far more courage than I possessed to have gone back to Battalion Headquarters with a flesh wound in my left leg, to report that Charlie Company had disappeared into the night somewhere in Tavoleto, whilst I had been hobbling my way back to find a soft bed in hospital. Of far more importance was my guilt about those tired, frightened soldiers who had been transformed into crazy, blood-thirsty men, for whom death meant little. I had taunted them into such a state of mind—how could I now walk away and leave them to their fate ?

Rambahadur and the company runner, Rifleman Jagatbahadur Rai, stayed behind as my escort. Gingerly I got to my feet to find that, using my tommy gun as a walking stick, I could hobble slowly for-ward. By this time 8 Platoon had followed the sound of the battle ; we went after them. We reached the outskirts of the village and even-tually met Jemedar Sherbahadur and some of his platoon crouched below a high wall, which appeared to segregate the Church tower and a few other buildings from the rest of the village. I asked what was happening.

'' We met no opposition, Sahib, on our way here. As you can hear 9 platoon is somewhere in the street over on our right. I have had no contact with them but obviously they are having a hell of a battle. I don't know where 7 Platoon has gone—the street on our left seems to be quiet. And there are still Germans inside the Church Keep because they fired at us when we were doubling towards this wall''.

'' Where the hell did this wall come from ? They didn't tell us about this ; it was not shown on the air photo—does it go right round ?''

'' As far as we know, yes. I have sent a patrol up the west street to see if there is an entrance there. Don't worry Sahib, we've checked that tank over there, it has been knocked out !''

Behind us was a self-propelled gun mounted on a tank chassis. I do not know whether the artillery bombardment had killed the crew or whether Jemedar Jitbahadur's Platoon had knocked it out when they burst into the village to enter houses on the eastern side. It was heart-ening to learn that someone had removed that ' beast' from the battle.

Under the wall, I began to take stock of the position, realising that we could not wait there for ever while a chaotic battle was waged without abatement. Who was friend and who was foe on our right ? It was an impossible question to answer. While I watched and listened it was evident that Germans and Gurkhas were fighting a deadly battle in the houses without knowing who was where. Control had been lost on both sides and I am certain that a high proportion of casual-ties—and there were many—was caused by ' own' bullets. Something had to be done.

My two escorts, Rambahadur and Jagatbahadur, were sent across to try and locate OC 9 Platoon, Jemedar Jitbahadur. If they found him he was to be told that his men were to disengage as soon as possible, unless there was a definite chance of clearing the whole street. Off the riflemen went on their difficult, dangerous mission. Meanwhile, Jemedar Sherbahadur led a patrol up the west street in an attempt to find 7 Platoon who had disappeared into the night. And another section from 8 Platoon tried to find a way into the Church tower in an attempt to silence the German snipers who were firing at us from above, making our position most unhealthy.

During a long eventful night, time meant nothing, nor can I recall how many hours we waited under the Church tower, protected to a certain extent by that wall. First to come back was Rambahadur on his own. His companion, Jagatbahadur, had disappeared somewhere on the other side of the street nor had he been able to locate OC 9 Platoon. Naik Chaturdhoj Limbu thought that the Jemedar Sahib was a few houses ahead but no one really knew who was where or what was happening. As I was listening to Rambahadur's report, Jemedar Sherbahadur arrived back from his patrol. The left hand street, the one on the west was completely clear : no enemy had been encountered but of 7 Platoon there had been no sign whatever. Sherbahadur's theory was that after finding that sector of the village comparatively undefended, 7 Platoon had wheeled back and joined A Company outside Tavoleto. There was no evidence to support his statement but subsequent events were to show that his assessment was correct in all respects. The Germans in the western houses had been unnerved by Able Company's attack launched after 11 p.m. Then, the screaming banshees of 7 Platoon descended on them and, after token resistance, the defenders had fled into the night. After clearing his street, Jemedar Abidal had reached his objective ; rightly or wrongly he was chary about his platoon remaining north of Tavoleto on its own so moving westwards, they joined up with A Company and temporarily took instructions from Major Moreton.

In the early hours of 3 September all this, of course, was not known to us as we crouched below the wall. The intensity of 9 Platoon's battle on our right continued ; it was absolute bedlam and many men who died or were wounded were hit by their own side. Listening to the curses and shouts it was hard to realise that we, Germans, Gurkhas and British, all belonged to the same family of humanity, striving for the same goals to better ourselves, instead of throwing ourselves into a torment of bloody destruction like animals possessed by black fury. Somehow I had to stop it, to retrieve the remaining soldiers of 9 Platoon before they all perished. But how ?

There were three alternatives, but whether I considered them in any detail in 1944, I cannot recall. Firstly, we could reinforce Jibahadur using 8 Platoon and Company Headquarters, in the hope that the extra men might be able to clear the last pockets of German defenders. In daylight I am sure this would have been the best and only solution, Now it was quite impractical because with friend and foe intermingled the extra men would only have added to the confusion rather than resolving it. The second alternative was to advance to the north of the village, to the objective we had selected off the air photos for Phase II. For many reasons this appealed to me but the obvious danger was that, with 7 Platoon missing and 9 Platoon still held in the village, we would be out on our own, vulnerable and defenceless in the open. And finally, the safest course open to us was to move to the west and join A Company. Jemedar Sherbahadur urged me to adopt the last course but I felt that we could best help 9 Platoon by moving north to take up a position, even if we stayed until daylight only, that might deter German reinforcements from trickling back into Tavoleto. After much indecision, I decided to do that.

Once more, the unfortunate but intrepid Rambahadur doubled across the street to contact 9 Platoon and tell them that we were moving on to our Phase II objective. 9 Platoon was to disengage as soon as this was proved possible and move north to join us—or alternatively, if dawn was approaching, they were to join A Company on our left. Rambahadur was away for a few minutes only ; once again he had met Naik Chaturdhoj who promised to relay the message on to his commander, Jendur Jitbahadur Rai.

Jemedar Sherbahadur Sunwar led our motley party through the empty street on the west of the Church tower. We numbered about twenty : some men from 8 Platoon had become casualties while, unbeknown to us, others had been sucked into 9 Platoon's battle My leg was throbbing viciously so that walking or hobbling was a painful business, I needed Rambahadur's arm as well as using my tommy gun as a walking stick. As far as possible we hugged the wall below the Church following it to the north end of the village, afraid that snipers in the tower above might see us. Eventually we had to cross the street but fortunately no one fired at us. Then through some back gardens and out into a field, away from the village of death. In the dark it was impossible to know whether we had selected a good tactical position. We had to stop because I could not go any further without being carried. Jemedar Sherbahadur formed us into a small tight perimeter realising that the Germans might attack us from any direction, including Tavoleto itself.

It was half past three. I am sure about this because Jemedar Sherbahadur wrote it in his report after the battle was over. After a few minutes the isolation of our position became more and more apparent. To add to the noise behind us in the village, came the the sounds of more firing from A Company's area. Soon, with good reason we felt that the Hosts of Midian were prowling all around us. Loss of blood added to shock made me weak and incapable of thinking very clearly. More and more did I wonder what we were achieving by staying where we were : the Germans, however saw to it that our journey to the north was not to be in vain and, as it transpired, not without tactical benefits in the successful outcome of the battle for the village.

The men on my right whispered that they had seen figures moving. Should they or should they not fire ? " If the Germans are moving towards the village then you must fire ", was the instruction passed from man to man to the section commander concerned. A few minutes later our bren gun opened up. The Germans went to ground. In the confusion it was impossible to say how many had been hit but the machine gun fire achieved its object. The enemy abandoned their attempt to reach the village and decided to attack us instead. They fired a few Verey lights above us, presumably trying to find out how strong we were. We opened up with all our weapons but soon ammunition was running short ; Sherbahadur controlled the fire of a few designated individuals, ordering everyone else to conserve their last few rounds in case the Germans tried to rush us. This they did not do but for a few minutes they were close enough to shower us with stick grenades. Although their stick ' bombs' did not have the lethal devastating effect of our hand grenades, in an encounter like the one we had in the field north of Tavoleto they could hit us while we had nothing that could be used in retaliation. During the clash, which lasted fifteen to twenty minutes, we lost two men killed and three more wounded. The Germans were so close we could do nothing except stay where we were and fight it out—to have moved would have invited annihilation and the wounded, including myself, would have had no option but to remain where they were. Whether the Germans thought that we were a bigger force than we were or were impressed by our determination to stand and fight, I know not : in the end they broke off the engagement and moved away to the north, away from us and away from the remainder of their garrison in Tavoleto.

I did not need Jemedar Sherbahadur's urgent plea that we should pull back at once ; I had already come to the same conclusion. Our task had been done and as the faint glimmerings of dawn appeared, we realised that we would be out in the open, vulnerable to mortar and gun fire as soon as the light improved. I told the Jemedar Sahib to take complete charge because I was feeling light headed with pain, not wholly responsible and not really worried whether I lived or died. Not surprisingly, therefore, I cannot remember how we managed to trickle back to join our friends in A Company

A Company had dug in below the road connecting Auditore and Tavoleto, using natural ditches as protection against the enemy mortars which had began to be active. Not only did we find Abidal's platoon but also a handful of survivors from 9 Platoon including Jemedar Jitbahadur Rai : in addition, we were greeted by Subedar

Krishnabahadur who had survived several adventures before reaching A Company. Krishnabahadur had been commanding the composite platoon of Charlie Company, taking orders from A Company's Major Moreton. When I met Moreton in his half constructed trench, he took one look at me and recommended that Charlie Company, or its remnants, should stay under his command. I thought that I had agreed readily with the suggestion but, when we next met, three months later, Moreton said I had been delirious and had tried to scramble out of the trench, shouting that I would take a patrol into Tavoleto, to rescue the missing members of 9 Platoon. It is a blank page as far as I am concerned but Moreton's account has the ring of truth about it.

As dawn broke there was still intermittent firing in the village on our right. Subedar Krishnabahadur reported that Charlie Company mustered less than fifty all ranks with a dozen of these wounded, awaiting evacuation to the rear. The wounded were a real problem for Moreton because he anticipated a counter attack at a time when he was woefully short of men, and he could not spare valuable men to escort the wounded back to the RAP. Eventually soldiers from D Company came forward but as the enemy mortaring intensified, the evacuation took a considerable time. About half a dozen men had been severely wounded and these were sent as and when stretcher-bearers were available. Moreton tried to persuade me to leave but my small wound in the leg was trivial compared with the pain being suffered so stoically and uncomplainingly by the badly wounded Gurkha soldiers.

Prior to leaving A Company's position, we had to endure yet another dose of German mortaring. As there was insufficient room for Moreton and myself in his small trench, I decided that the least valuable part of my body was the wounded left leg so this stuck out in the open, much to my companions' amusement.

I have said that this is not an official or unofficial history and for that reason, I have resisted the temptation to draw on the excellent accounts in the 7th Gurkha Rifles Regimental history My recollections are so hazy about the morning of 3 September that an exception has been made. The official account states that : ' The two companies burdened with many wounded men and more than a hundred prisoners were persistently shelled and mortared and being almost out of ammunition had many moments of anxiety'.

The shells, the bombs and the wounded : all these were part of that grim struggle to retain the western end of Tavoleto. The total of prisoners seems inordinately high but later I was to learn that many Germans were keen to surrender after first light, before they were blasted out of the village and exterminated by the next wave of Gurkha attackers, supported by tanks.

When I left Moreton and his depleted double company, the worst seemed to be over. Rambahadur came with me in a group which consisted of several German prisoners, three walking wounded, and a small number of Gurkha escorts. Rambahadur supported me as best he could until two Germans volunteered to carry me. Linking hands to make a ' walking seat', they did not have much difficulty in lifting and holding my light weight frame. At the time it all seemed natural, two able bodied men helping someone who had been temporarily incapacitated ; afterwards in hospital, I recalled how I had hobbled into the village with the help of a tommy gun, only to return by favour of two burly German prisoners. Another memory was that the prisoners, inadequately guarded by two or three Gurkhas, had ample opportunity to escape especially when, lower in the valley, some shells landed nearby. In varying degrees of speed according to our agility, we went to ground ; when it was over the Gurkhas were as surprised as I was to find that all our charges were present and correct.

"I'm glad to see you are still here. I thought you would make a run for it"; I said to the English speaking German by my side.

" Why escape ? We have lost the war. And anyway I do not want to face your Indians again".

" Gurkhas, not Indians. They will be very angry if you call them Indians. They come from Nepal, which is north of India".

The German grinned, translated my remarks to his companion, and then commented, " No wonder. We had heard about the Gurkhas. Now they look very harmless".

A few minutes later the so called inoffensive Gurkhas found themselves protecting the band of German prisoners from irate Italian refugess, the real occupants of Taveleto. We came across them hiding in the low ground, a group of excited men, women and children who had fled before the battle for the village had begun. In sorrow and fear they had witnessed their homes and possessions being pounded to rubble and dust. It was us, the Allies, who had done so, but their wrath was for the hated Tedeski who had decided to make Tavoleto a strong hold, who had fought to hold it against heavy odds and by doing so, had ensured its total destruction. They rushed towards us shaking their fists and waving sticks. I shouted to the Gurkhas that it was their duty to protect the prisoners even if it meant opening fire. The sight of tommy guns and kukris was enough—the Italians let us go, contenting themselves with shouting curses at the Germans as they walked back into captivity.

At the Regimental Aid Post (RAP) there were several wounded men waiting for Gerald Sausman to do what he could before arranging for their evacuation back for further treatment. In the morning light he looked desperately tired and dirty but presumably I presented an even more sorry sight. He smiled when he saw me and came over. took off the field dressing, and looked at the long, angry wound, ' Not too serious' he said, ' but I expect the MRS at Urbino will have to operate because it badly needs cleaning and much blood has been lost'. He told me that Alan Howard wanted to speak to me ; a message was sent to tell the intelligence Officer that I was in the RAP. The doctor cleaned up the wound, put on another temporary bandage and gave me a morphia injection while I waited for Alan to arrive.

The last thing that I expected was to be congratulated on the attack. To me it had been a complete shambles, confused, badly planned at all levels, with nothing appearing to have gone according to expectations. Being a wiser man now, with some knowledge of military history, I realise that most of the so called classical battles of the past must have been viewed in the same light by those who participated in them. I felt guilty at having so aroused Charlie Company, that my control of events thereafter had been flimsy and, on occasions, non-existent. Alan found me dejected, bitter, and very worried about the handful of men who had remained to fight it out with the Germans in the houses in the east street. To my amazement he greeted me with fulsome praise, adding that the Colonel was extremely pleased with what we had achieved. It had been a long night for Battalion Headquarters because, without any radio contact with C Company, not a single report had been received after nine o' clock in the evening, for over twelve hours. When the wounded had trickled back from A and C Companies in the early hours of the morning, their stories had been garbled, contradictory, often inaccurate, and in most cases highly coloured. The first reports had indicated that I had been killed, then later one had it that I had been wounded but had disappeared. Alan could not stay long as the Battalion was still battling to retain possession of Tavoleto and the ridge running to the west. Wishing me luck, he dashed off to rejoin the Colonel who had gone on ahead, towards the village.

Before saying goodbye to Gerald, I promised to write from whatever Base Hospital I was bound for and asked him to tell Alan something that had been forgotten in our hurried conversation ; the gallantry of certain individuals merited immediate decorations which meant writing citations at the first convenient place and time. I promised that I would include these in my first letter to Gerald for him to pass on to Alan thereafter. " Okay, Birdie. You lucky devil, two or three months rest for a cushy wound. Perhaps I may be joining you ".

I never saw Gerald Sausman again. Some thirteen years later, when revisiting the battle areas with my wife, purely by accident did I come across his gravestone in a neat, well kept war cemetery, not far from where the gallant doctor died, tending the wounded in full view of the Germans. That is the way he would have wished to die—looking after his patients.

The short time I spent at the MRS was like a nightmare. Ambulances and jeeps continued to unload the wounded of many nationalities until there was a long line of stretchers, each with a man covered by a brown army blanket ; some were dying and the majority were in the throes of pain and suffering. There was the smell of death in that long corridor which could not be hidden by antiseptics and the combined stench of dirty unwashed men. The small staff of doctors and orderlies could not cope with the sudden influx of shattered bodies. In theory the MRS was intended to categorise patients, prepare them for evacuation and only in dire emergencies was life giving surgery to be attempted. The first few days of the Gothic Line battles had been costly in lives and the tally of wounded had exceeded all planning expectations. Extra surgeons had been rushed up to the MRS at Urbino because for many patients, a delay in surgery would have meant certain death. Medical orderlies did their best to look after us but, poor devils, they were rushed off their feet by calls and pleas from various directions. Eventually my stretcher was carried inside the improvised operating theatre. The tired RAMC major undid my bandage and looked at the wound. When were you hit, he asked. I told him. In that case, he said, we had better clean you up here.

That was to be my first visit to any operating theatre. I wish it had been my last ! At that time, I was so tired with my leg throbbing with pain that the thought of temporary oblivion under an anaesthetic was something to be welcomed, not feared. The crashing of shells, the excited screams, the battle for that hell spot called Tavoleto with men fighting like crazy animals, all was forgotten before I had counted up to ten, with the weary surgeon poised to begin yet another of the dozens of operations he was to carry out without sleep or rest.

Next day the evacuation back to the Base hospitals began in earnest. We were loaded on an American ambulance plane at Ancona. I can remember that it was a very hot day and after our stretchers had been put aboard the transport aircraft, sweat rolled off our bodies as the engines roared, then spluttered and died. They left us inside ; soon it was like a fiery furnace. Some patients grumbled, others moaned and one man fainted with the heat. Eventually the fault in the plane was rectified and an attractive American nurse came back on board. Everyone alright, she asked. In an embarrassed way a British soldier indicated that his bladder was bursting. The nurse produced a bottle for him, where upon to her obvious annoyance we all asked for the same article. Numerous cups of tea consumed during a long wait at the airfield had taken a natural course through our bodies. Unfortunately the American girl thought that the general cry of ' Can I have a bottle too, Nurse' was suspiciously like an organised leg pull. She took some convincing : the look of contentment on all our faces as we eased our aching bladders must have convinced her that she was indeed an angel of mercy.

For me, and for those who were on that plane, the battle for the Gothic Line was over. But not for my Battalion. Tavoleto was but the first of several hard fought operations that faced them in the Autumn of 1944. The village, or what remained of it, was finally cleared by B Company supported by tanks as I was being evacuated to the MRS. Inside the village B Company found only dead and dying Gurkhas and Germans. Tavoleto had fallen but at a cost. The official story related that ' The attack on Tavoleto succeeded because in the face of great difficulties, all ranks pressed resolutely forward, searching out and killing the enemy. Casualties were heavy. C Company alone lost 44 men killed and wounded'.

During 1973, nearly thirty years after, the village I revisited was a flourishing one, bearing no resemblance to the ruins we fought for in the war. In the place of the original Church tower there is now an up to date 3-star hotel. When the proprietors realised that the ' Nepalesi' were the descendants of those who had wrested their village from the Germans back in 1944, they insisted on producing numerous flagons of white chianti for the coach load of Gurkhas who had arrived to ' take over' the hotel. After a short speech from the Commanding Officer of the present day 7th Gurkha Rifles, the men sang popular traditional Nepalese songs in the large hotel dining hall. Interested Italian spectators appeared, eager to ask questions, brimful of curiosity.

For me it was a most moving experience to be sitting in a room below the old Church, listening to the young Gurkha soldiers singing under candlelight, their faces flushed with wine and the joy of living. Tavoleto is a happy village now, with much charm, set in the peaceful Italian countryside, away from tourists and busy roads.

The night in September 1944 seemed unreal, even in my memory. I turned my attention to the impromptu party.

It was a memorable evening.

Chapter 5

HOSPITAL

IT would be idle to pretend that I would have remembered very much about life in 93 General Hospital near Barletta, in South Italy, had it not been for letters written from there to my mother. Enforced stays in hospitals elsewhere at other times have a far more vivid place in my memory ; my leg wound was a flesh one only, although aggravated by the unavoidable time lag before I was evacuated to the MRS. Subsequent injuries in later wars were to be more serious—unfortunately.

On 7 September my first letter : ' Another long silence broken, sooner than I expected, as I have left the lads up with it all. Yes, Mum don't get worried—Gerry got me but nothing to lose a lot of sleep about. I have been doing Company Commander for quite some time now, a big job for a junior officer and I was just getting promotion when this happened. A major at 21 would have been something, even if only for two months, but by the time I get back, other officers, senior to me, will be out of hospital too. Still I had the honour of leading C Company into three attacks and being successful every time. Not that the last one was a picnic as some fine men were killed and wounded'.

' I was hit by a German machine gun through the left calf but no injury has been done to the bone. They cannot tell for a day or two whether the muscle has been affected. This they will find out when the surgeon skin grafts over the wound. If the muscle is unaffected then it should not be a very long job. At the time it did not hurt too much and I waited until we had taken our objective before moving back'.

' I am bored with hospital already although only arriving here yesterday. We were evacuated from the front by air which was not really appreciated by most but certainly quicker and less bumpy than the Italian roads. The trouble with a leg wound is that you are not allowed to do anything—even going to the toilet—without asking for the aid of an orderly'.

' I feel out of it now, never having missed a day since first going up to join the Battalion at Cassino. Most of us who joined in March have now been wounded or evacuated through sickness. It was inevitable really and it could have been far more serious as far as I am concerned. Don't worry about this scratch (I won't call it a wound as you would imagine that my left leg is hanging off !)'.

Fortunately that letter arrived on the same day as an official telegram from the War Office which stated in bare terms that, ' Lieutenant E. D. Smith had been wounded in action and evacuated to hospital'. My parents were saved many hours of agonising worry by the speedy arrival of the air letter.

Hospital life for those of us who were not severely wounded was a frustrating business. The Barletta Hospital was badly overcrowded and, at first, extra beds had to be placed in the officers' ward ; it was impossible to separate those who were dying and those who had lost limbs from the many who were but temporarily incapacitated by moderate, light injuries. I have but two memories, one tragic and the other light hearted.

After I had been in hospital a day, a young Sapper subaltern was brought in with a shattered leg and put in a bed next to mine, behind screens. I could not see his face but he spoke to me in a cheerful voice before being taken away for a major operation. Later, at night, he recovered from the anaesthetic and with the nursing staff rushed off their feet, there was no one there when his pain-wracked brain drifted back into conciousness. Before being taken to the operating theatre, the boy had not realised that he was about to lose his leg below the knee. During the night the shocked realisation gradually came to him ; it moved me to tears when he began to moan, ' Wheres' my leg, where's my leg, they've taken off my leg'. What can one say in such circumstances ? I could stand it no longer ; I rang and kept ringing the bell above my head until the QA Sister appeared. A screen was put round the subaltern and the duty doctor gave him an injection to help him withstand the pain, to dull the shock of his personal tragedy. When I woke up in the morning the bed was empty ; the Sister explained that he had been moved into a ward on his own. I believe that he lived although I never saw him again.

The next occupant of that bed was an Irish captain who, inevitably, was called Paddy within an hour of his arrival. He was a cheerful extrovert, a Catholic from Eire who soon told us that we were a lot of English bastards and as soon as the war with the Germans was over he intended rejoining the Irish Republican Army to fight us once more. We did not know whether he was being serious or not. No matter, Paddy was like a tonic in our ward as he bubbled over with exuberance and good humour which helped to pass the time, and made us laugh. Like all hospitals, 93 General woke up all the patients in the very early hours of the morning to start the tedious daily routine, so beloved by the medical profession—or its staff members anyway. Paddy was a violent objector and on the second day swore that the night Sister, before she handed over next morning would be taught a lesson if she tried to arouse him from his slumbers only to be given a bed bath and other fussy ministrations. You watch me, he boasted, I will fix that Florence Nightingale.

Next morning came ; the night Sister, a young Scots girl with auburn hair and high colouring so typical of her race, began rousing us with bowls of water and sharp-tasting thermometers pushed into sleepy reluctant mouths. Eventually she came to the recumbent Paddy. He was shaken into wakefulness although I am sure he had only been pretending to be asleep.

'' Get up, Captain Paddy. I'm not going to give you a bowl of water—you can go to the bathroom while I straighten your bed''.

He grinned, then said : '' Sorry, Sister, I cannot get up. You know I was dreaming about you when you shook me. It was a wonderful, romantic dream. Unfortunately a certain part of me is feeling very cheeky at the moment''—and as if to emphasise the point, he pushed up the blanket between his legs.

The poor girl blushed furiously while we crowed with laughter. She disappeared and Paddy chortled with delight at his easy victory. Alas, he had only won the first round. A minute later, a Major QA sailed into the ward. She was a formidable figure of a woman, generously proportioned above and in front, which made her appear like a galleon under way. She stormed up to Paddy's bed.

'' Good morning, Captain Paddy. I hear you have a problem. I cannot have the routine of this ward upset by cheeky members, however big, however small''.

And having delivered the warning, to Paddy's surprise she whipped back the bedclothes and delivered a sharp slap on his cheeky, offending member. The laughter in the ward gave the final victory to the formidable lady. Next morning, Paddy went off to the bathroom.

About a week later I was bemoaning the lack of mail, the boredom but, most of all, being confined to my bed. ' The dressing on my leg, put on after the last operation, is not to be moved until ten days have elapsed—however it has been giving very little pain so that I am quite optimistic about it all. Taking all in all, I expect to be walking around in about a week and, possibly, after a further three weeks at a rehabilitation centre, back with the Battalion by the third week of October. By that time the war might be very different although Gerry is fighting as hard as ever in this country. I think, however, that it is his last effort, an effort of despair because his retreat across the Lombardy Plain will be a dangerous undertaking with our Air Forces '.

I had plenty time to think about the future and in my letters showed a deep concern for the Gurkhas who had been such loyal soldiers in Italy, Africa and Burma. ' What of the future ? I cannot see our (Fourth) Division being disbanded after the fall of Germany. Gurkha troops are too valuable and too good in the jungle for them to be left out of the final stages of the Japanese war. Like all British officers in Gurkha battalions, I dislike the readiness to sacrifice Gurkha soldiers in difficult tasks rather than using British troops. Casualties of the Gurkhas are higher than any country in the British Empire, in proportion to Nepal's tiny population of little over ten million people'. (That was an underestimate of the Nepalese population, even in 1944). ' Most people think of them as Indians—which is quite wrong as their country, Nepal, is an independant one and has never allowed us (British) to cross their borders. Although they like us, they do not trust us in case we exploit them'.

I do not understand what was meant by that statement. It is possible that I felt that if the Nepalese Government opened their country to foreigners, then the ruling Rana regime might fall as indeed, happened in the early nineteen fifties.

' Our men say that their farms are deserted save for old men and their womenfolk. About a quarter of the population is voluntarily fighting in this war for us. It is a fact not realised by many people at home who talk about sacrifices. Coloured the Gurkhas may be but some of the whitest, bravest, and most honest men I have met have been Gurkhas'.

Obvious I was in the grip of a deep, strong emotion to have written in such a way to my parents. The letter ended : ' Well, lecture ends. I am sorry. I did not mean to write all the above but I was carried away. I am very well and, please, do not worry'.

I wonder now what was meant by the accusation that Great Britain was exploiting the Gurkhas of Nepal or indeed from where I obtained such an impression. Was it from one of the many wounded Gurkha soldiers in the hospital, who might have expressed bitter feelings ? Possibly : I do remember one NCO who had lost an arm ; his spirits were so low that the doctors feared for his life. Trying to restore his faith in the future proved to be an exacting and, in the end, impossible task.

My next letter, written towards the end of September, returned to the subject that was worrying me most, the future. ' Well, Mum, the war years are nearing an end and I can now claim to have some overseas service behind me. I don't have any illusions about my immediate future either—the European war is but a phase in my personal war effort or rather the Indian Army's war effort. Granted we have to return to India ; to give our men much needed leave ; to re-equip ; to train in jungles after long periods spent in mountains. All this will take months. Only if Japan falls quickly can we avoid it'.

' Frankly I am not keen about it all—the jungle, Japs and another dose of war, such a combination does not thrill my young imagination in the slightest. The Far East is a long way from Great Britain. People in England will take far less interest in the capture of say Manila, than they would in the fall of Antwerp or Aachen. Germany' defeat will start a cry : '' We have finished it, holidays for all at last''. OK, they have deserved it but many thousands of troops will have to fight on. Nothing will '' brown them off'' more than if they read about England returning to peace-time conditions, of men being demobilised and obtaining well paid jobs, while they fight to capture tracts of jungle which mean nothing to them. There must be no half measures. The United States has done most of the dirty work for us in the Far East. Now we have to be prepared to do our share or we will lose trade, national prestige and a large chunk of the Empire when it is all over'.

' I feel strongly about it all. I know that troops who are fighting in France and Italy will be disgusted about having to go out to the East. But men in the 14th Army have been fighting under terrible conditions for over two years. They have had old, antiquated weapons, little air support and, worst of all, little interest has been taken in them by the people at home. They have had a rough deal and a far tougher time than the troops in France or even Italy. Although the struggle in France may be tough at times, the country has a decent climate. Italy, hard going from Sicily to the north, does have many amenities to offer'.

' I do not regret coming abroad. Many things have been open to me which I would never have seen if I had remained in England under peace time conditions. Certainly I have had many varied experiences and learnt a lot. I have seen many parts of the world and have met hundreds of people in the normal casual army manner. But, I have seen enough of war to convince me of its utter stupidity. Yes, and many other things. Most important of all, I have had, responsibility thrust at me since I was twenty and mens' lives have been put in my hands !

That particular letter went on and on ; I do not intend to quote other parts except the ending.

' I would never have chosen the Army as a career had it not been for the war but I am now considering it as a profession. I have no business or other qualifications and lack a University education. And, I have not used my brain since I was seventeen ! (The letter was written at the old age of twenty-one !). ' The idea of studying at University does not attract me. The Army in peacetime offers many attractions : an out-of-door life, opportunities for sport and travel. I agree that the pay is not generous but there is a measure of security. Finally, and probably most important of all, I like and admire the Gurkhas, I speak their language, and the peace time stations in India for the Brigade are always in the Hills. Having said all that, I must admit that the Army irritates me in many ways ; in peace time it may be an aimless life without any object to work for and I'm not sure that I want to spend many years in India. Others may enthuse about India but to me it is a dirty and unattractive country, With the majority of the population none too friendly.'

The serious tone of the letter caused me to add a postscript ; ' I am ashamed at the seriousness of my letter, in parts it reads like a political lecture ! Forgive me as I do not always think and talk like that. Perhaps I am over pessimistic about the war with Japan. I hope so. Get ready to take down the black out'.

It had been a great relief to my parents to receive the first air mail letter before the official telegram arrived, notifying them about my wound. ' I was hoping that this might happen as I knew the telegram would worry you ; after all, the classification of wounded could mean anything, from a leg missing to a scratch like mine. Unfortunately my leg is not healing as quickly as I would like, although the bullet did not hit the muscles. The surgeon had a three and a half inch wound to stitch up. Normally this would not have presented a big problem but he had to tackle it in Barletta, five days after I was hit. The stitches are out but the gap has not closed and the wound is still discharging. It is nothing to worry about but I may have to be in bed longer than I originally anticipated. It is most annoying as I feel as well as ever and the leg gives me no pain or trouble'.

That day I hobbled round to visit some of the wounded Gurkhas in their ward. This prompted the few lines added as a postscript : ' I am proud to be with the Gurkhas—all British officers are. No troops in the world can attack with such fervour and gusto as the Gurkhas. They are the tops !'.

From those letters it is clear that two days later, and without any warning, a few officers were moved from Barletta across Italy to a British Hospital near Pompeii. ' As you can see I have moved from the east coast to the west. We came by train to Naples and from there by ambulance to this hospital, which is not far from the famous ruins. The journey was not too bad although I was ordered to lie on a stretcher. This annoyed me as I feel perfectly fit and can walk without any pain and do not limp'.

' The doctor at this hospital has yet to see my leg so that it is impossible to give you any indication of how long I may be here. You will remember how my cuts, boils etc. always took a long time to heal when I was a boy. I fear that this wound is playing the same game'. And then a tinge of sadness about being away from the

Battalion. "Eighth Army reaches the Plain, speedy advance expected", so say the papers. Just my luck to be present when we were advancing less than a hundred yards a day and then to miss the quick sweep forward when life is easy and there is very little fighting'.

Later I added that a doctor had inspected my leg and had not been over happy. 'I was not meant to read the official writing on my medical card at the end of my bed, but I peeped at it when the Sister was out of the Ward. "Unhealthy oscilations, with green pus discharges". I fear that half the wound is still open'.

103 British General Hospital was not working under such pressure as the Barletta one had been so that the staff had more time to look after their patients. During this period I wrote a letter every day : most of them referred, again and again to the progress being made by my leg. It was being obstinately slow. In addition, many times did I bewail the fact that no news had been received from the Battalion, 'I don't even know if my attack on 3 September was a success or not'. Then followed a welcome switch to another topic. 'We the British are willing to pay sixteen million pounds a day on the war but will grudgingly spend less than half that for those who fought, when peace comes. Let us hope that such selfish attitudes will disappear. After all it is not communism to express the hope that every living person shall have food and work and the right to own a decent home. It is just common sense. I have met hundreds of what we used to call 'The Working Class' and they all expect these basic requirements when the war is over. They will get them, too, even if it hurts a few members of the over worked rich'. The idealism of youth and, perhaps, the pendulum has swung too far in the other direction ? My long suffering parents were subjected to numerous serious lectures, hence : 'Apologies for writing about such topics but honestly there is nothing to write about in hospital. All I do is eat large meals, sleep and worry about my leg, and about my friends in the Battalion'. That particular letter was signed off by, ' A very impatient patient'.

As day succeeded day, there continued to be silence from my friends who, unbeknown to me, were engaged in a series of tough battles. The only way to find out what was happening at the sharp end was to return there but, regrettably the 'leg' was proving to be uncooperative. 'The doctors are discussing whether a skin graft will be necessary. They are afraid that the long scar may break down as soon as I take any violent excercise. Anyway no decision will be made until Thursday'. And then back to thoughts about those Germans, ' Gerry seems to be holding everywhere. No one can deny that he has courage and high morale in spite of many defeats and our intensified bombing. We must have killed thousands of their civilians, too'.

Next day, from a letter, it seems that I was allowed to hobble around outside the ward. That meant a search for clothes: 'I haven't any clothes at all with me which is a trifle depressing. I hope my wee orderly keeps an eye on my stuff but I have a horrible presentiment that Rambahadur 'bought it' after I left. Why I should have this feeling, I don't know. I have had no mail or any message from the Battalion'. A few lines later came a postscript, 'It is ironical really. Here I write a letter a day when I have no news but when with the Battalion I write so irregularly although each day in the lines brings forth many incidents of note. On reflection, however, perhaps it is just as well that I do not record or remember them'.

The feeling of guilt about being away from the fighting stirred me into adding: 'NAAFI today, but we are not allowed to draw our beer or whisky ration while we are in hospital. It seems wrong, really, especially when the lads in the Battalion will not draw my share. Goodness knows who is drinking my ration—I know I'm not!' The irritation passed because next day, a Sunday, there was a big inspection of wounds:

'Hooray, mine has dried up and closed at both ends with but one small opening in the middle. The stitching should prevent a scar so eventually I will have nothing to show the world for all that trouble. I won't be able to show my children what a brave man their Dad was!'. My sojourn in hospital was coming to an end: 'From here I expect to be sent to a convalescent home where I may spend from two to three weeks before returning to the Battalion. Indeed in a month from now I might well be back with my friends. I am looking forward to seeing my pals again. You can't beat the spirit of comradeship especially after men have been in action together. Everyone seems far less selfish'.

Life indeed was looking up and, I was not confined to the Hospital ward. 'Yesterday a party of us were taken for a short trip in the Bay of Naples. Fortunately the sun shone and we had a most enjoyable three hours in the fresh air, landing near a place not far from the beaches over which a famous battle was fought last year (Salerno). I admired the rugged scenery with the mountains seemingly climbing straight up from the sea. It certainly is beautiful and now I understand why so many tourists visit this area in peace time. If only southern Italy was not so dirty and the people so lazy. What a contrast to north Italy and Rome.

Later that day I and others moved to a convalescent home in Sorrento. 'It is grand here. I was lucky and brought fine weather with me and have certainly picked up in health and colour again. My leg is completely healed although more scarred than I had anticipated '. ' The Bay of Naples with Capri standing boldly against the evening sky : the gaunt and unlovely Vesuvious, and the white city of Naples which can be seen so clearly across the water—all these make Sorrento an ideal place for a convalescent home. It is a memorable experience to wander around the old town. Naples is beautiful from a distance but not so pleasant when you walk through the narrow back streets. Nothing like Rome for cleanliness, and the buildings, old and new, are not of the same standard.

' The Convalescent home is well run, with good beds, nice rooms and adequate food. In peace time it is a hotel and as a consequence there are excellent lounges, dining rooms and so on. I can honestly say that I have enjoyed my stay here, it has probably been the most pleasant week I have spent in Italy so far. Tomorrow I am going to the opera in Naples which should be interesting. Thereafter, on the following day, I may be on my way back to the north. As to when I will reach the Battalion is problematical as I may have to go via various reinfoicement camps. I gather that my appointment in the Battalion has been filled by another officer. The Battalion is enjoying a well earned rest from the rigours of the Gothic Line '.

There were other letters but there was much repetition in them. Each letter revealed a measure of guilt about being away from my friends although, many years later, it is not easy to understand why such feelings tormented me. That there was a deep desire to find out what happened after the Tavoleto battle was understandable ; no one wrote from the Battalion so that I did not know whether Charlie Company's attack had earned praise or disapproval from the people that mattered, the men who followed me and charged into the village after their tempers had been roused. A complete lack of communication with Battalion Headquarters had protected me from pressures from higher headquarters so that, in the Convalescent home, I did not worry about the opinions of senior officers ; all I sought and awaited was the judgement of the men I had commanded for such a short time. Thus, an impatient desire to rejoin the Battalion can be explained. Not one of the letters reveals any keenness to return to full scale active service : I had had my fill of fighting but, if the 7th Gurkha Rifles were due to return to the front line once more, then my place was with them.

The few days spent in Sorrento were pleasant ones, chiefly as it was late autumn and the weather was glorious. Each day I wandered slowly around the old town at a gentle pace, but increasing the distance until my leg began to throb. For the first time in nine months there was leisure and an opportunity to appreciate the beautiful country around Sorrento. There were, of course, no tourists and we could stroll down the narrow streets without discomfort and without being jostled by holiday makers. The feeling of peace was absolute ; the temptation to stay longer was very great.

The morning came when about a dozen officers had to present themselves to the doctor for a verdict on their future. I cannot remember what he looked like or his rank or name. But I can recall his opening words, as if he had said them to me yesterday.

" Lieutenant Smith. I wonder what category you belong to ?"

Hopefully, I replied, " Category ' A ', fit to return to my unit, I trust".

" Not quite what I meant, Smith. I have been here six months and I now classify all officers into two categories : and, unfortunately both types try to fool me. The first category consists of those who are fit to go back to their units but have no desire to do so—they are the ' Lotus eaters' so they complain of aches and pains. And in the second category are those who should not go back but are determined to do so even though unhealed wounds may suffer as a result of their keenness. Everyone who comes on this weekly review is a dishonest guy as far as I am concerned ".

I hesitated before saying : " Honestly, Doctor, I believe that I'm in a third category ; my leg has healed and irrespective of my feelings I should go back to my Battalion".

The doctor grunted, took off the bandages and examined the long scar. It was impossible for him to miss the fact that about an inch in the middle had still not closed. One or two questions followed as to how far I had walked, had there been any pain—did the left leg feel weaker than the other one ? He sighed in exasperation and then went to his desk. All was quiet except for the scratching of his pen. His face gave no indication as to what the verdict was going to be, but I feared the worst. Was it to mean another visit to the Hospital ?

" Right", he said, " What is the name of your Regimental medical officer ?"

I told him. " Okay. Your diagnosis was wrong—you are definitely in the second category of officers, trying to fool me into saying that you are fit to return to active service. However, I will play ball with you if you promise to obey my instructions. I have written a note to your Medical Officer to say that for three months you must be on light duty—and I do mean light duty. Is there any sedentary post you could fill in the Battalion ?"

I told him that 4th Division had been withdrawn for a rest so that there could well be certain administrative jobs that I could do He grinned and put his hand out.

" Good luck, Smith. And don't tear that piece of paper up because another copy will be sent through the official mail to your doctor".

I was free to go next day and I did not intend to waste any time. There were two ways of returning to one's unit in north Italy. The official method was to report in person to the nearest reinforcement camp, armed with the medical discharge slip, and put oneself at the mercy of 'the machine'. Clearly this was the safest way of getting back. Nevertheless there were inherent dangers ; if the Battalion was showing a full complement of officers on its daily strength returns, then the unfortunates waiting in the reinforcement pipeline could be diverted elsewhere or, horror of horrors, find themselves being given appointments in one of the reinforcement camps. The alternative was to bypass the system, to hitch hike from Naples, through Rome and thence up to the north to wherever the Division was located. Many had done this in the past and, as a result, Army Headquarters had issued stern warnings promising punishments for future transgressors. On the notice board in the Convalescent Home there was a copy of the order. Moreover, the problem was made more difficult because we could not communicate with our units : with a war on, no one was going to waste official signals about the movements of junior officers, even if we felt that we were important people.

Being catious by nature my original intention was to obey orders. Four of us were taken by ambulance into Naples to the officers' shop so that we could buy some clothing and I purchased a second-hand battle dress blouse with the 4th Indian Division's sign—the red Eagle—on the arms : this familiar insignia was far more important than officers' 'pips' and my assessment was shared by three New Zealanders who stopped their 15 cwt. truck to hail me as I was walking down the street. Where are you going, they asked. I told them. Fine, they said, we, too, have been wounded and are now going back to join our division which is next to yours. Jump in. And I did, without any further thought.

Long before the Italian campaign began, and many months before I joined the Battalion, 2 New Zealand Division and 4 Indian Division had fought side by in many actions against Italians and Germans. The bond between the Divisions was a close one, based on mutual admiration and respect and the reputation of both Divisions was high indeed. Not that three New Zealand soldiers, one lance corporal and two privates, worried about such high-falutin ideas—they saw my red 'Shite Hawk' on the battle dress blouse and treated me as if I was a fellow countryman. It would be stretching the truth if I pretended to remember their names. The Lance Corporal was a huge man, well over six foot and inevitably he answered to the unoriginal name of Tiny.

As far as I can recall it took us three days to reach our destinations, probably because we lost a few hours in Rome. My companions decided to have a party and reluctantly I tagged along because I did not want them to disappear for ever in the great city. Tiny drank more vino that night than I have ever seen anyone drink at any time in my life : he kept going but his two mates passed out. Tiny was furious with them because the Pom (myself) was still on his feet but he had not noticed that I had been dragging my heels from the very start and, in fact, had consumed little compared with his two inebriated pals. Fortunately, perhaps, thirty years and the vino I drank present an impenetrable curtain over the rest of the night in Rome.

Next morning we set off, none of us in a cheerful mood, as we were suffering remorse caused by lively hangovers. Tiny decided that we would rotate the duties as driver, his co-partner as navigator with the map, and the other two resting in the back of the vehicle. This proposition alarmed me because I had never driven a 15 cwt. before, and was certain that I would stall the engine. Without suspecting that I was an officer, they made some pretty pungent remarks about the British army not teaching soldiers to drive. To stop their wisecracks I volunteered to do two stints as navigator which was greeted with acclaim, because a wrong turning taken or bad navigation could be blamed on the man with the map. After an hour of silence, broken by a few bad tempered curses, Tiny decided that we all needed some vino. Best cure for hangovers, he explained. On that day he may have been right because after a few drinks, the conversation became more cheerful and I found the three of them engaging and likeable fellows. Time passed ; soon I realised that my most important task was to keep whoever was driving awake as the hot afternoon sun beat down which, together with the vino fumes, invited sleep.

It may have been the second day, possibly in the morning when, without warning, the engine of the vehicle spluttered and coughed in a tired fashion and conked out. The language of my companions was vitriolic, original and delivered with complete sincerity. The three men knew how to drive but no one had any knowledge of what went on under the bonnet. Nevertheless, various parts of the truck's anatomy were probed, checked and scrutinised but to no avail. For the first time in my life, I heard someone use the well known British soldier's four lettered word as an adjective, noun and verb—just three words, but how expressive was Tiny's final verdict : " The f——g f——s' f——d ".

The three Kiwis set off for the nearest village, to drink vino and drown their sorrows. I decided it was safer to stay as sentry with the vehicle rather than get involved in another night's carousing with the boys. After they had gone round the next bend in the road, and idly to pass the time, I slipped into the drivers seat, switched on the ignition, and pressed the starter. The engine's voice rang out strong and true. Not daring to switch off I let out the clutch and in bottom gear set out after the three New Zealanders. I did not change up in case the engine stalled.

Outside the village I caught up with the Kiwis : their faces were quite a study :

" Pom, you're a bloody marvel, why didn't you tell us you were a mechanic ?"

They jumped in, all thought of another bout of vino drinking forgotten. And away we went to the north once more.

Although I volunteered to go with them to their Division, the boys would not hear of it. No, Pom, we will deliver you to your unit. You are a bloody marvel as a mechanic, we owe it to you. They were a little puzzled when I told them that I wanted to go to the 7th Gurkha Rifles and assumed, I imagine, that I was a British soldier attached to the Gurkhas. Any way, nothing was said until we arrived at my Battalion's location. Tiny was driving, with me sitting next to him. The 4th Indian Division was in a rest area, several miles behind and away from the front line. I do not remember its exact location.

Our vehicle was stopped by a Gurkha sentry. He peered in the front window, then there was mutual recognition. He was a rifleman from Jemedar Abidal's Platoon. Forgetting the normal conventions about protocol when on guard, he shouted : " Eh Sathi Ho, Hamro Esmith Sahib ayo" (" Oh friends, our Smith Sahib has come back").

His mates flocked out of the improvised guard room and dashed towards us, with broad welcoming smiles on their faces. They were all from Charlie Company. The Naik remembered to salute first but the riflemen pumped my hand with delight before he remembered that, although my battledress blouse had no badges of rank on it, prior to being wounded I had been an officer. The Kiwis watched this in amazement, indeed I had forgotten about them. Remembering my manners, I turned and walked back to the truck. " Why didn't you tell us you were a bloody officer ? To think that we have been travelling with the top brass for three days", came from one of them.

Tiny was equally outspoken. With a smile, his comment was. " Well, don't expect a bloody salute from me until you're properly dressed, Lieutenant Sahib"—and then roared with laughter. The Gurkhas joined in the general laughter, not fully understanding our exchanges but realising that the giant New Zealander was pulling my leg. We asked them to stay for a drink but they declined—their Division lay to the north, near the front line. I thanked them for the lift and their cheerful company. Tiny's farewell comment was, " I'm glad you travelled as a Pom and not as a bloody officer, otherwise we wouldn't have left you behind as vehicle escort—and who would have started the vehicle ? Your Johnies obviously like you—I guess you're a good bloke''. Then off they went, my three friends of the road whose names I cannot recall but whose company I do not forget.

Thence to the Officers' Mess where I was met by a wide variety of greetings, ranging from surprise to comments about Errol Flynn returning to finish off the war. Why had I not written, asked the Adjutant. He took the very words out of my mouth, why had they left me in the dark ? Obviously, somewhere in Italy were many letters which had been sent in good faith, which never arrived. Eager to learn what had happened during the two months, a string of questions came from me rather than from the relaxed group of friends. The Division had been pulled out and was due to sail for Greece in three or four weeks time. That was the main item of news. It was surprising, and unexpected, and momentarily knocked me off balance Was our, my, part in the war over then ? Would there be no more days and nights when fear tightened my belly until I wanted to scream ? When I had tried to encourage the Gurkha soldiers, knowing that my own fund of boldness had no reserves left, an overdraft which needed time and rest before the next challenge could be met with any confidenec. '' Don't look so gloomy, Birdie. The war is over. We're going to Greece, and the Germans are pulling out, or so we're told. And the Greek girls are every bit as glamorous as the Eyties. Have a drink—you look as if you need one. In fact, you can pay for the round as you're improperly dressed, Rifleman Smith. Orderly...''.

At some stage in the merry evening someone told me that Gerald Sausman had been killed just after the battle for Tavoleto had been won. As some eight weeks had elapsed, the other officers had passed from grief to acceptance in the casual inevitable way of wartime. The news stunned me, however, because Gerald had been closer to me than anyone else, especially after Gunnar had died. The happy reunion in the Mess turned sour. It was as if someone had turned off the tap marked happiness: a deep weariness choked my excitement, turning day into night. It was time to leave, before I behaved in an un-British way : to have revealed deep sorrow in public, at a party in the Mess, would have been a social ' black'.

The Adjutant accompanied me outside realising that the unexpected news about Gerald's death had knocked me sideways. We chatted about the future until I remembered the citations that had been written shortly after I had reached the Barletta Hospital. These had been sent in an envelope to Gerald Sausman with a short note : what had happened to my letter ? Had someone opened it after Gerald had been killed ? No, was the reply, no citations had been submitted for Charlie Company after Tavoleto. The Colonel had wondered why I had not produced any names but was hoping that this could be remedied now.

" My God, why the hell did I send it to Gerald ? Ninety men attack a village on their own, we lose over fifty and not a single man gets a decoration. Norman, this is terrible news. What can we do ?"

" We'll do our best. I suggest you write the citations out as soon as you can and I'll ask the Colonel to send them to Brigade Head-quarters by tomorrow night. We mustn't waste time, though, because everyone is thinking about our future in Greece and not about past battles".

My guilt was not made any easier when Norman hinted that I had been put in for an unspecified decoration by the Colonel. He warned me not to pass the news on to anyone. What an anti-climax and how ironical, when, for months past, my daydreams had in-cluded E. D. Smith winning an award for gallantry at the head of a company of Gurkha soldiers. And now, there was no anticipation in my heart : and there could not be any until I was satisfied that some of those who went into Tavoleto would have their gallantry recog-nised. Those citations were re-written that evening, with the help of the Company Gurkha officers. For them, in fact, it was not so easy because Tavoleto had been but one battle for Charlie Company ; in the fighting further north other bloody actions had been contested although the outcome had not always been successful. Regrettably decorations are rarely handed out with any generosity when a company is surrounded and has to withdraw under severe pressure— as C Company did, from off the Scorticata Ridge two weeks after Tavoleto had been captured.

After finishing the citations, I wrote the first letter for nearly three weeks to my long suffering parents, who had guessed that the silence had been due to my travelling rather than active service conditions. Eventually the letter appeared in early November : ' I am sorry I haven't managed to scribble anything for so long but I have been travelling up and down this fair land. The journey wasn't all it could have been because the vehicle I was travelling in broke down but you will not believe it—I was the guy who started it. All I did was to press the starter after others had fiddled around to no avail '.

' I was delighted to meet the Battalion again after nearly two months of silence and found it very changed. Especially my old C Company which, I gather, continued with their great work on three occasions after I left but unfortunately did not escape lightly. In fact, I was shocked when I saw the large number of new faces. Our doctor was killed two days after I was wounded—a grand bloke who was always in the thick of it, who never stopped work however tired he was and however dangerous the shelling. I gather the new doctor also did magnificent work in the later stages. Yes, our Battalion has a great reputation in a wonderful Division'.

' I'm afraid all my kit was missing, so the Colonel is letting me go back to Rome in order to buy a few things. I've been attached to my old Company but without a specific job until my leg heals properly. I'm not ambitious and as our Battalion has many officers present, senior to myself, I am not worrying unduly'.

Re-reading the letters, and to my surprise now, I find that I had added an uncharacteristic postscript : ' However, I have been in more sticky parties than most'.

Next day, after a long sleep, I surveyed my available kit which amounted to shaving gear and the dirty clothes I was still wearing after the journey. Where had my clothes gone, and where was Rambahadur ? The disappearance of the one was connected with the death of the other. The company runner, Rifleman Jagatbahadur Rai, came to break the news to me. He apologised that the Sahib had no kit left ; abruptly I broke in to say that my few clothes and wordly possessions could be replaced, the loss was nothing. But Ramu, how had Ramu been killed ? Gently his best friend told me how Charlie Company had virtually been surrounded on the Scorticato Ridge when the order to withdraw had been received ; those who stayed till the end did so to cover the withdrawal of the earlier platoons. Ramu was in the last section which ran out of ammunition as the Germans pressed home and closed with them. Next day when the position had been recaptured, Ramu was found with two dead Germans near him, both of whom had died after being hacked by his bloodstained Kukri. It took Jagat some time to tell me the story, then he burst into tears. Tears unnerve me at any time, and all I could do was pat him on the back and assure him that my grief for Rambahadur was as deep as his. When he had recovered some of his composure, Jagatbahadur said that Subedar Krishnabahadur had detailed him as my orderly. What did I want him to do ? At that time I had nothing, no kit, no shoes to clean, but I was touched by the Subedar's kindly thought. " Fine, Jagat, I am delighted. But I may not stay with Charlie Company long. When we reach Greece I may be given another job to do. What then ?"

" No matter Sahib, wherever you go I will go. Ramu was with you in A Company, in the Patrol Platoon and then with Charlie Company. I will do the same".

And he did—until, for compassionate reasons, Jagatbahadur left the army when the Battalion returned to India in 1946.

Later that day, Subedar Krishnabahadur Gurung asked if I would join them in the evening for a quiet drink. He apologised for the informality of the invitation because they had not known that I would arrive ; anyway, C Company was on Battalion duties, consequently not many men could be present that evening. We chatted about other things before he left, promising to collect me at six o' clock.

There were less than fifty men assembled to meet me when Krishnabahadur and I arrived in the company lines. At first I wondered if I had come to the wrong company. There were so many new faces and, dear God, how young they looked. Sixteen year olds pretending to be men. Then, gradually, I saw there were a few familiar faces after all. Abidal with a broad smile, Jemedar Sherbahadur Sunwar, the Sergeant Major, the Quartermaster Budhiraj Limbu who had brought up the cannister containing my rations at Tavoleto, Naik Chaturdhoj. I went from one friend to another shaking hands, as they showed their delight at seeing me again, while I thanked the Almighty that they had been spared after so much, to be still there as the backbone of Charlie Company.

Before the drinking began, before the bhat (curry and rice) appeared, Subedar Krishnabahadur clapped his hands, shouted for silence and said : '' I'm not going to make a speech. I've apologised to the Sahib for the fact that some of the company are on guard and others have gone on leave to Rome. All I want to say is, welcome back Sahib ; you have come back to your home''. Applause—my eyes were damp with tears. Yes, indeed, I was home again bound by the same ties of duty, affection and loyalty to the Regiment as those friends of mine who smiled at me that night in November, 1944.

Many years later, twenty to be precise, I was to leave that home, and that same Regiment. The occasion was honoured by a Pipe Band, ready to play nostalgic music as I left the lines. I was seated in a wheelchair while, one by one, Gurkha soldiers, and their wives, garlanded me with freshly picked and woven flowers ; many hesitated before shaking my left hand. My right sleeve was empty.

It was a sad, and a most moving occasion. But that was to be in a land far away from Italy.

In 1964 the Gurkha's motto, '' It is better to die than be a coward'' helped to sustain me during a period of much trial, pain and suffering.

But that is another story, in another war.

Chapter 6

THE YEAR OF THE BULLETS ENDS IN GREECE

IN 1945, the late Aneurin Bevan attacked the Government for their intervention and policy in Greece. One of the statements made by that eloquent critic was, "A Gurkha is to the Greek as the Moor is to the Spaniard". I remember the real anger in our Mess when this was read out to us—there was certainly no doubt that A. Bevan, Esq., was like a red flag to the British officers thereafter. He was called ' Urinal' Bevan by us all. Perhaps he was surprised to hear that Gurkha soldiers had even gone to Greece. You may be, too—hence this epilogue to my 1944.

During the move down Italy everybody was in high spirits. There were regrets that the plains of the north still lay ahead and to others had been given the honour of the final coup-de-grace. But yet unspoken but very much in our minds, was the realisation that the war in Europe was drawing to a close. The Battalion had seen its fair share of fighting and as peace seemed imminent, so did our interest in survival increase. To Greece, therefore, where the German Occupation forces were already being withdrawn, where we expected to be greeted as liberators and to spend an easy, pleasant interlude until Germany surrendered.

I think that we were almost across the Adriatic before anyone mentioned the possibility of trouble and we heard for the first time the term ELAS. British Intelligence agents, on several occasions during the German occupation, had received useful support from the ELAS (Communists) and, in return had arranged to hand over quantities of arms and ammunition to their Greek Allies. Such a situation was to be repeated in Malaya. We failed to appreciate that the Communists' long term aid was to avoid a large scale confrontation with their German/Japanese conquerors so that they could be in a position to take over power during the vacuum at the time of liberation. The Communists may preach detente but never do they disarm nor are they deflected from their ultimate aim, which is to establish their way of life throughout the world.

My first letter from Greece commented : ' I cannot say much about this country as we have only just arrived and it has been raining heavily ever since. As we steamed towards our destination, the hills and the coast line from our ship looked like the Lebanon with the rugged mountains and occasional green plain. Whoever said that there would be no trouble over here ? It all seems so stupid and unnecessary at such a late stage in the war. Violence has begun—the Communist factions are using the arms originally given them by us to be used against the Germans. They are attempting to intimidate the average Greek citizen into accepting their system of Government. At the moment things are pretty tense and all eyes are on the struggle which is taking place in Athens. Will ELAS or the British win ?'

As we, the 7th Gurkhas, landed at Patras we were greeted with the news that ELAS had already taken over many important areas in Athens, Salonika and, indeed, in Patras. Our holiday never started and, a few days before Christmas 1944, we were living in an atmosphere that needed but a spark to ignite passions and result in open warfare.

In the town the ELAS were in great strength and they made this fact as obvious as possible, both to the local inhabitants and to us, 11 Brigade. Armed men in different and varying degrees of uniform swaggered around, some smiling arrogantly, others looking like sullen gypsies on the rampage. As we sat down to dinner in the Officers' Mess, an ELAS machine gun from the top floor of the house on the opposite side of the street was trained on our dining table. No one lingered over his meal, not even on Christmas day ! In retaliation or even self defence, ' They' (up above), allowed us no scope whatever as a very strict set of rules had been laid down.

To young men whose last few months had been spent in the full scale conflict of Italy, such restrictions were irksome and appeared to be devoid of meaning, but events were to prove our Commander, Brigadier John Hunt, (Later Sir John of Everest fame), right in every respect. We, in 11 Brigade, were weak in numbers and equipment whereas the Greek communists mustered the equivalent of two divisions in and around Patras. John Hunt had one policy—to keep negotiating even if it meant temporary appeasement. ' Jaw Jaw not War War'. At our lowly level we were puzzled but more of this later. We felt frustrated and restricted in all our activities, nothing was to be done to upset the Greeks. However, every situation produces the man and we in the 7th Gurkhas had two for this tense, somewhat gloomy occasion. Matt Mulloy and Moreton had their own theories on how to live in wartime and John Hunt's edicts were contrary to their ideas which had been put into practice many times, in Beirut, Cairo, and in the large cities of Italy. So to Greece.

Their first public display was to drive a Jeep up the steps of the local Coliseum after a rather protracted Sunday curry lunch. This display proved very popular with the locals especially as Matt stood or swayed with an angelic smile on his face. Smiles at Brigade HQ, albeit cold ones ! But the next display by our two jokers led to their departure from Patras. ELAS decided to hold a dance to which their erstwhile British comrades were not invited. Not until the heavenly twins arrived with Matt, as ever, to the fore. With a hand inside his jacket, he turned to Moreton and in a conspiratoral but loud whisper asked where he should throw ' it'. ' It' was, in fact, an orange, but no one stopped to find out. The dance hall emptied, the women shrieked, men jumped out of windows while our two comedians collapsed with laughter. It was their swansong and life was never the same without them.

I must digress for a paragraph to let you know about a battle that I lost. The citations written with such speed after I rejoined the Battalion in North Italy, arrived back from Brigade headquarters minutes before we sailed from Italy. The short cryptic note told the Colonel to resubmit them in Greece since it was too late for them to be processed, especially as the Battalion was due to embark. After we reached Patras, the same citations were sent up to HQ Land Forces in Athens only for an equally blunt reply to be received : too late, not our business, you (7GR) should have submitted these before, through your parent formation in Italy. Impasse, I was hearbroken as well as angry. In addition there was a sense of personal guilt and the letter to my parents reveals the reason.

' I don't think that I told you that '' They'' put me in for some decoration on account of our attack in September. I gather it takes about three months to come through but it does not mean that it is certain to do so. I know what the Colonel has put me in for but I am not saying anything as it appears most unlikely that I shall get it. Anyway, these awards always seem unfair to me. Some of the bravest of our men have nothing to show for their courage on many occasions. Now that I have seen how decorations are awarded, and to whom they are given, I am under no illusions about decorations—awards mean little except on rare occasions'.

Yes, it seemed as if but one person in Charlie Company would re-ceive an award for Tavoleto—myself. Instead of anticipating with joy the possible announcement of my ' gong' I found myself dreading it. How could I face C Company after the news had been promulgated ? In particular Naik Chaturdhoj Limbu deserved an award of the. highest order for his magnificent patrol before we attacked the village. I complained to Desmond : eventually he suggested that if a single shot was fired in Greece at ' or near' Chaturdhoj, then his name should be re-submitted for another award, using the present to put right the injustice of the past.

The Major commanding C Company agreed to do his best. By an extraordinary coincidence the one NCO in the company who was in the thick of the trouble, during skirmishes near Patras, was Naik

Chaturdhoj Limbu. No story had to be falsified, no fabrications had to be invented : he won his decoration in Greece for outstanding bravery—but it should have been a bar to the IDSM he ' won' at Tavoleto on 2 September, 1944.

C Company's last battle did not take place until the turn of the year. Days passed with Greek and British alike, tense, suspicious and listening to the daily, even hourly, broadcasts from Athens. By now it was clear that the future of Greece was being decided in the capital city—the victors there would eventually rule the whole country. Such indeed was John Hunt's daily theme when he talked to his ELAS counterpart. '' Why fight here ? If your side wins in Athens then your victory here can be achieved without any bloodshed. If we win, then. . . . . ''

Unbeknown to his opponents and those of us away from the seat of power, the British planned to ship a brigade, with supporting tanks, from Athens to Patras as soon as the struggle there had been satisfactorily resolved. Suddenly this came to pass. Athens was ours and 139 Brigade began landing at Patras with ships of the Royal Navy in support. It was a glorious, a stirring sight for us, if not for our opponents. The tables were turned and our quiet Brigadier became a commander who meant business and this involved the complete disbandment of the ELAS forces facing us.

An ultimatum was given, to be clear of a certain demarcated line by the following morning or face the consequences. Amazed and disheartened by the news from Athens, and unpleasantly shaken by the sudden display of British strength, the local High Command agreed, but stated they could not guarantee compliance by their more fanatical subordinates. 7th Gurkha Rifles was told to take up positions along the hills to the east of Patras by the following morning and to disarm anyone found within the prohibited sector. No one in the Battalion really expected any fighting but nevertheless the operation was planned on the assumption that some members of ELAS might refuse to obey their superiors' instructions.

My three months of light duty was nearly over but at that time there was no vacant appointment in the Battalion. Consequently, I volunteered to accompany my old friends in Charlie Company as an observer, without any official role to play. The Gurkha officers did not greet my offer with any obvious enthusiasm : they told their company commander that whenever I went with them, C Company invariably seemed to run into trouble, and to end up in the stickiest of situations. However, this excursion appeared to be a formality and I was allowed to travel with their vehicles along the road from where the Battalion's cross country march was due to begin.

It was bitterly cold, Greece in winter would make a brass monkey's accoutrements rattle. Sitting in the back of an open jeep, next to the driver because the vehicle was being driven by one of the two British officers in front, the bitter test of endurance became one of survival in the cold. I think we would have perished had it not been for the fact that the Gurkha produced a blanket under which we were forced to keep our heads, obtaining some measure of warmth from each others' bodies. When I shivered violently, the Gurkha said : " Don't worry Sahib, you'll be alright. The ELAS won't fight on a night like this. Don't be frightened", then to my surprise he momentarily held my hand. Huffily in slight embarrassment, I maintained that it was the cold that was making me shiver, not fear.

But the Gurkha, whose name I forget, had really irritated me because his intuition was correct ; I was afraid, the black snake of fear was in my stomach, and in my ears were the shouts and screams of Tavoleto once more. Why had I volunteered for this operation when it was nothing to do with me ? It was too late. We had arrived at our debussing point. Stiffly I climbed out and to the driver's surprise, returned the compliment by shaking his hand.

Then began a long walk over difficult country. It was a dark night but the men in front set a stirring pace which got our circulation going. I had no responsibility whatever which meant that I could concentrate on walking without having to worry about anything else. After about an hour my left leg began to hurt but considering that the the going was hard, the terrain rough, then it stood up to the ordeal remarkably well.

Before the morning light came, a tired footsore company was sitting in platoon positions overlooking one of the possible valley exits from the Plain of Patras. Soon the early rays of light revealed a large body of men moving towards us. Not daring to let them get near enough to over-run us by sheer weight of numbers, we opened fire at long range, hoping that many would waver, throw down their arms and evaporate back to their peaceful occupations. We followed Napoleon's dictum : ' On s'engage : puis on voit'. I sat by two Gurkha riflemen who were manning a Bren gun, watching as they fired at a group of ELAS, working their way through a cemetery ; the little dots appeared to drop like ninepins. The LMG gunner shouted jubilantly : " We've got them Sahib. You have a go : let us see what your shooting is like". After I had settled behind the gun there was no movement for a few seconds, then first here, then there, the little ants appeared, doubling forward to throw themselves down behind cover again. I pressed the trigger, fired a burst and saw one or two drop. In my excitement and at such a range it was easy to forget that the targets were human beings with the bullets ripping holes in them, killing them, maiming them. And did they want to attack us or were they trying to escape from the British infantry and tanks as they landed behind them in the Bay of Patras ? The game palled. I had had enough : the Gurkha gunner took his place behind the LMG once more.

'' But you were shooting well, Sahib. I was using your binoculars and you hit at least four men'', reported his number two in surprise. '' Perhaps, but it is your job, not mine'', and I took hold of my binoculars to search the area below us. That day I learned a lesson : even if men go to ground under fire, and they appear to be ' sitting ducks', it does not necessarily mean that they are dead or wounded — and to assume so is the height of folly. We did this only to find ourselves under severe pressure in less than an hour. Those Greeks had courage but fortunately for us their leadership was poor, many of their weapons were antiquated, and ammunition was in short supply. Gradually we assumed control, disarmed many, captured scores of sullen and dejected men.

We were winning—but were we ? I cannot recall why Naik Chaturdhoj was the senior person in 7 Platoon's location. No matter. Soon his men were under heavy pressure from all sides, Gurkha and Greek fought with courage until neither side had any ammunition left. At such a crucial moment another platoon from Charlie Company arrived to drive off the Greeks, and to find that 7 platoon had already used kukris when the Greeks charged the position. Chaturdhoj, about five foot zero and a half inches in height, had killed five ELAS soldiers with his kukri, leading a counter attack at a time when the battle appeared to be lost. One Gurkha soldier was killed and another badly wounded but the story of the battle was soon to be known all over the Peloponese. The Gurkha and his kukri became a legend overnight.

That little action was the last of the Battalion's fighting in Europe as well as being the end of 1944, ' the year of bullets'. For us, in C Company, was the prize of a delightful hamlet by the name of Claus, a centre of the local wine industry. We claimed it only to be told that Battalion Headquarters had decided to set themselves up there. Possession was ours, however, as Claus lay below us after the fighting was over. A compromise solution saw us being nominated reserve company, sharing the excellent accommodation with our superiors. Brigade Headquarters tried to move in on the act too, but no quarter was given. They still managed to visit us on many pretexts but by that time we had hidden the best of the wine in the Battalion reserve ammunition store.

And so the fighting was over although in 1945 we were to face one or two tense moments elsewhere, particularly after we moved first to Salonica, thence north to the Yugoslav border, to be based near the town of Kilkis. The story of the following year in Greece does not form part of this book. Suffice to say that when we left for India, Gurkhas and Greeks, poor in worldly goods but both races tough and proud, the truest of comrades when danger threatens, had become great friends. So much for the prophecy of Aneurin Bevan ! When we left for India, there was the satisfaction that no longer did Red Flags fly over Greece.

Early in 1945 the last paragraph of a letter to my parents reported : ' I suppose that this will arrive around the New Year. Let us hope that this will be the last year of the war. We are all getting very war weary which is not surprising.

I don't know whether you will have heard from the War Office about my DSO. This may be your first news. I was very lucky and consider that the award should have gone to the whole of C Company rather than to me personally. Our CO got one as well. Well, Happy New Year, Eric'.

So, what I feared came to pass, I as Company Commander, my Battalion Commander as well as our Brigade Commander, were all honoured with the DSO—but not a single Gurkha soldier from Charlie Company Many years later after the majority of the survivors had returned to their homes and farms in Nepal, when the war was but a memory, they were honoured in an indirect manner. The 7th Gurkha Rifles received Tavoleto as a battle honour : rare indeed for a single unit to be given such an honour and probably unique for a rifle company to have won the honour virtually on its own.

As time passed I learnt to accept the meagre rewards and unfortunate outcome. Remembering the words of the poet Housman, " I lived in a world I never made". But I had learnt a little about leadership of men in the face of horror and death. I had seen that Gurkhas can be brave one day and cowards the next : that the motto, " It is better to die than be a coward" is an ideal that is rarely attained, even by Gurkha soldiers themselves.

But, of one thing I was certain, it is wise to be on the same side as the Gurkhas.